HOLLYWOOD WITH A SMILE

HOLLYWOOD WITH A SMILE

Sandra de Bruin
with
Dean Brierly

BearManor Media

2022

HOLLYWOOD WITH A SMILE
© 2022 *Sandra de Bruin with Dean Brierly*

Published in the United States of America by:

BearManor Media

4700 Millenia Blvd.
Suite 175 PMB 90497
Orlando, FL 32839

bearmanormedia.com

Printed in the United States.

Typesetting and layout by BearManor Media
Cover design by Andrius Krasuckas and Dean Brierly

ISBN—979-8-88771-028-0

TABLE OF CONTENTS

DEDICATION

This book is dedicated to all the hard-working and dedicated actresses and actors—unsung and successful—who, through their talent and creativity, elevate the entertainment industry. Their work helps provide us a respite from reality, and inspires us to pursue and live out our own dreams.

ACKNOWLEDGMENTS

Many people have been encouraging and helpful in the process of pulling these many stories together in one book. A special tribute goes to Catherine Duncan and Bareda (Barri) Clark for putting up with me and my frequent writer's block and computer anxiety. Also, a special acknowledgment to Lori Ageno-Brierly, Dean's wife, for quietly forsaking social engagements while we wrote. To these three ladies and all our friends, our deepest thanks.

Special accolades to the following: Nick Lyons, author of the newly released *Fire in the Straw*, and co-writer and editor of the many trout-fishing books that he and my Dad wrote. His guidance and friendship throughout my writing career has been invaluable. Steven Stiefel, co-author of *Tomorrow's Flight*, as well as numerous magazine articles and scripts. Steven's creativity is boundless. Joe Jordan, author of *Robert Wise: The Motion Pictures*, the fascinating, in-depth critical assessment of this legendary director's career. Joe's encouragement and professional advice are appreciated. We are so indebted to these three men for giving of their time, energy, and creativity. Without them, *Hollywood With A Smile* would still be a pipe dream, not a book.

Last but not least, a sincere thanks to our publisher, Ben Ohmart, for his guidance and precise advice on grammar and format. He should teach correct writing in every school in America.

In closing, once again, THANK YOU!

PROLOGUE

Ah, the sweet smell of success,
That's Hollywood at its very best.
But that's so rarely true.
Success in Tinseltown is for the very few.

There's the never-ending flow,
Of actors as they come and go.
Their winning dreams they can't sustain,
So home they go, their hopes in flames.

Yet for some their dreams come true.
They land a role; it's a film debut.
Their talent and careers take flight.
They reach the sun and dazzling heights.

This book is about famous stars whom I have met,
Some personal tales about that iconic set.
Read the fun and tender stories I have scribed.
You'll laugh and cry and maybe sigh.

Here are my tales of show-biz life,

Existing with a bit of strife.

But I smiled and stuck it out.

Thanks to my friends and a bit of clout.

Sit back and enjoy the read.

This book will easily fuel your need

To thrive and love the life you chase.

May it help you find your special place.

Success is failure turned inside out,

The silver lining of the clouds of doubt.

Remember that, I do implore.

Read it twice, I'll say no more.

HARRY BELAFONTE

1927–

Every teenage girl has an idol, a crush on some handsome, talented superstar, be it an athlete, singer, or movie star. I was no exception.

(Harry Belafonte, the King of Calypso, began his illustrious career in the early 1950s. He made several television appearances before starring in the hit musical Carmen Jones *(1954). But his calypso and Caribbean records (yep, the vinyl ones) soon made him one of the era's biggest superstars, an entertainment king on par with the likes of Elvis Presley and Frank Sinatra. Six feet tall, brown, and beautiful, the Jamaican-American singer, songwriter, and actor combined his musical talent with a powerful screen presence in such films as* Island in the Sun *(1957)—my favorite—*The World, the Flesh and the Devil *(1959),* Odds Against Tomorrow *(1959), and* The Player *(1992). He also made a number of significant guest-starring television performances. During the course of his career, Belafonte won three Grammy Awards (including one for Lifetime Achievement), an Emmy Award, and a Tony Award. He was the "Usher" of his era, talented, stylish, and charismatic. He was also a strong supporter of the Civil Rights Movement during the 1960s and one of Martin Luther King's closest confidants. To this day, in his ninth decade, he remains active in the movement for equality for all ethnicities.)*

Meeting Mr. Belafonte

It was a lovely New York City day in the spring of 1954. My mother had just parked our sturdy black Buick with big steel bumpers outside the garage where we stored it. This was located near our mid-Manhattan apartment on the West Side on 78th Street. She told me to wait in the car while she went inside to pay the monthly bill.

Mom had left the car on the street, so I slid over to the driver's seat and quietly waited, daydreaming and fantasizing about this and that. Suddenly, I was jolted from my reveries by a sharp bump. I spun my head around and saw a black sedan that had just exited the garage. The driver, obviously aware that he had hit our Buick, pulled abreast of our car, then swerved in front of it and parked. I expected some further reaction, but he just sat there, seemingly with no intention of getting out.

Being 14 years old and feeling cocky and in charge of any situation, as most 14-year-old kids are, I jumped out of our car and indignantly strode up to the driver. He turned his head as I approached, wearing an "I don't need this!" expression that momentarily stopped me in my tracks. After taking a deep breath, I leaned forward and looked directly at him.

Whoa! There was no mistaking him. It was Harry Belafonte, my first leaving-childhood-behind crush. Seated behind the wheel, gazing up at me with his chiseled features and hypnotic brown eyes, was the man who frequently inhabited my teenage romantic imagination. I couldn't move. My feet felt nailed to the pavement. Neither of us spoke. We just stared at one other as the seconds ticked by. A strange sort of energy seemed to hold us in thrall.

Harry Belafonte, singing, 1954.

I didn't know what to say or do. Suddenly, out of my mouth came, "I guess you can't drive as well as you sing!"

He paused, lowered his eyes, and, looking straight up at me, let out that wonderful "Ha!"—that inimitable combination of a laugh and a hiccup that often spiced up his calypso songs. A moment or three passed as I wondered whether I was awake or dreaming. Finally, my idol spoke.

"Sorry, my mind was elsewhere. Tell the garage to have any repairs done and charge it to my account. Have them contact me if they have any questions."

To be honest, I don't remember the exact words, because as it turned out, there was no damage to our Buick, not even a dent. In those days, bumpers were made of steel, not thermoplastics, and were impervious to that kind of minor collision.

My usual garrulousness had deserted me. All I could get out was a nervous, "Okay." But I still didn't move. I just stood rooted to the spot, gaping at him.

Finally, with what seemed liked compassionate understanding and a hint of a smile, he said, "Miss . . . what is your name?"

"Sandra," I timidly answered.

"Miss Sandra, can you step back? I need to get to my meeting. I'm already late!"

Those words brought me back to my senses. I reluctantly did as he asked, then watched as he drove away.

I never saw or met him again, but for weeks I floated on Cloud Nine, bragging to my friends about my unforgettable one-on-one with the King of Calypso.

As the years passed, I faithfully attended his concerts and played his calypso and Caribbean records over and over, to the point that my mother threatened to confiscate them if I didn't stop. I didn't, and to this day I still play the CDs.

I realize that Mr. Belafonte has probably long forgotten our Brief Encounter on the streets of New York City in 1954, but it doesn't matter. I have not. Fast forward 30 years. A friend and I were having coffee at a trendy coffee shop on Melrose Avenue in Hollywood, when she looked up, pointed to a table across the way, and whispered, "Hey, there's Shari Belafonte."

I spun my head around, just as I had in 1954. Sure enough, there was the beautiful daughter of my first crush, Harry Belafonte, enjoying a latte. Born the same year in which her father ran into my mom's car, she was a star in her own right: a model, writer, singer, and actress best known for her role on the 1980s television series *Hotel* (1983–1988). My heart quickened its pace, but I controlled my impulse to approach her and share my chance meeting with her father. By then my own career was going great. I had done *The Rockford Files* (1974–1980), *Barnaby*

Jones (1973–1980), and *The Tonight Show Starring Johnny Carson* (1962–1992), but it's kind of an unwritten rule for those of us in show biz to refrain from bothering celebrities when they are privately relaxing.

As the years have passed, however, I kind-of, sort-of wish I had. I think Shari would have enjoyed that narrative, and in a two degrees of separation way, it might have afforded me a vicarious reunion with the imposing, yet understanding, and still eminently crushable dreamboat in the black sedan.

FREDERICK COMBS

1935–1992

The actor Frederick Combs was one of the most intelligent, creative, and fascinating men I met during my Hollywood days. Ours was the most passionate, platonic relationship imaginable.

(Frederick Combs was known primarily as a theatre actor, making his Broadway debut in A Taste of Honey *in 1960, for which he received a Tony nomination. He next appeared in* The Lady of the Camellias *in 1965. He came to the public's attention in the acclaimed off-Broadway play* The Boys in the Band *in 1968, which was subsequently made into a 1970 film with the entire cast recreating their stage roles. Its groundbreaking portrayal of gay life made it a milestone in gay cinema. (Frederick once told me it was a difficult role to play because he could not find a reason why he would stay at such a terrible party.) He subsequently made a few made-for-TV movies and miniseries, but became bored and disenchanted. A prodigy of legendary acting teacher Uta Hagen, Frederick subsequently became a successful acting coach to the stars. In 1979, he founded the Actors' Lab, a scene-study class for working actors.)*

Love and Chaos and Life with Frederick

In or around 1986, I joined the YMCA in Hollywood and signed up for a bi-weekly dance/aerobics class that fit my dance background and promised much-needed exercise. Our group was led by a well-known older ballet artist. I kept to myself during the first class, but by the second session I began to take in the other participants. One guy stood out. Frederick Combs. He glided across the floor like a cat stalking its prey. He was mesmerizing.

After that workout, I joined a small group from class for a coffee get-together; among them was Frederic. After several of these coffee klatches, I learned about Frederick's Actors' Lab workshop. A month later, I was a member. Many wonderful things resulted from being part of the group, including an incredible friendship with the witty, talented, and fascinating Frederick Combs.

The Actors' Lab was an evening scene-study class. The participants ranged from talented to not-so-talented actors. Each week, most everyone did a two-person scene, after which Frederick would dissect it and give the actors dead-on pointers. During the following week, the actors would rehearse and incorporate Frederick's notes, with the end result being at least a fifty-percent improvement over the original performance. Of course, it depended on how skilled the actors were. My favorite scene partner, and soon best friend, was Jacqueline Schultz. She was amazing, and worked all the time.

Frederick ran a very professional class—be on time, know your lines, and no chewing gum—and the students loved him. On occasion, he would snap, like the time a young macho guy called him Fred. "My name is Frederick. Not Fred or Freddie. It's Frederick," he icily responded. Another time, a sexy gal unexpectedly turned her scene into a veritable porno show. Frederick studied her silently for a few moments, then quietly said, "You're obviously in the wrong theatre. You'll do well in a strip show on Hollywood Boulevard." She left that night, and never returned.

After class, a few of us, including Frederick, would go for coffee and/or drinks somewhere close to the theatre. It was during these wrap gatherings that Frederick and I became friends. Perhaps it was because we both were a bit older than most of the students, who were still chasing the Hollywood Dream. We had been there, done that.

Daytimes, Frederick busied himself with private coaching to stars like Rosemary Clooney (and family), soap opera stars, in-demand character actors, plus members of the Actors' Lab whenever anyone had upcoming auditions. He never seemed to stop working, but he was never too busy to not coach me before my auditions. Unlike his class notes, he would narrow in on every nuance of the character and the scene. Nine out of ten times, I would book the job.

In 1988, after several unhappily married years, I got a divorce. Frederick and I then became a platonic duo. During the years we were together, I did not have single a romantic relationship—with anyone. No man could top Frederick! We had dinner together, shopped together, and together attended his students' theater productions, which more often than not were paralyzing. But Frederick would always go backstage after the shows and say something encouraging. "You were amazing." "You've done it again." "The show wouldn't be the same without you." I didn't have it in me to be so benevolent, and usually waited for him in front of the theatre.

Frederick's thoughtfulness carried over into our personal relationship. Several days into a relentless Los Angeles heat wave, Frederick decided, or rather *insisted*, that I get a window air-conditioning unit for my bedroom. His adamancy may actually have been based on self-defense, since the undue heat and humidity had destroyed my sense of humor, heightened my sensitivity, and made my hair frizz—qualities that upset Frederick because he could only tolerate warm, witty, and beautiful.

Be that as it may, off we went hand-in-hand to a discount appliance store. I instantly spotted the ideal air conditioner, a small $300 unit, perfect for my bedroom. Frederick studied it for a moment, put his arm around me, and gently pulled me aside, emphatic that I get a bigger and better one. "You need it! You deserve it! It'll only be $100 more! Don't be cheap!"

Of course, I got the bigger and better unit. Who wants to be cheap? Unfortunately, bigger and better didn't fit into Frederick's sports car, so delivery had to be arranged and prepaid. Another $50! An hour or two later, it was delivered, but could not be installed. Neither Frederick nor I had remembered that there were security bars on the window that had to be removed so that the unit could hang out the window. The next day, a handyman arrived with special tools and removed the bars and set the unit in the window. Another $50.

That evening, with a great sense of accomplishment, I stood in front of my new air conditioner and turned the sucker on. There was a horrendous thump, followed by a blast of cold air. Suddenly, the *entire house* began to vibrate. For a split-second I thought I heard, "Thank you for flying American Airlines." Then, silence and an ominous calm. All the circuits had blown. I ran to the breaker box and threw the switches on again, only to turn around and find the house ablaze with electronic blinking red lights. Time Square was a distant second. Thirty seconds later, the sprinklers went off, and then *everything* went dead.

Somewhat hysterical, and not in the funny sense, I called Frederick and asked him to bring candles. He dutifully arrived an hour later, after searching all over West Hollywood for beeswax candles. Regular candles wouldn't do, of course. They drip!

A few days and I lost track of how many phone calls later, an electrician arrived. The cure-all: a $10,000 central cooling system. The immediate remedy: add a separate circuit for the air conditioner at $300 plus parts. The latter was, of course, my choice. Thanks to my dear Frederick, approximately $1,000 later I finally had an air conditioner. By then, the heat wave had passed.

Our social outings also extended to numerous upscale gay and straight parties. Frederick would always insist on parking his sporty Triumph facing out so we could make a quick escape when he'd had enough, which was usually an hour or so after arriving. Frederick had given up alcohol and drugs, and without them found this kind of socializing difficult. One time, he brought along a pipe to smoke, just to have something to fiddle with, and then proceeded to dump his pipe ashes into the host's late wife's urn. However, he invariably came through with witty stories and outrageous remarks. Everyone loved him.

One downer to our relationship was that every Christmas Frederick would go to Hawaii. He would pack a bathing suit, a beach towel, and his little sparkling fold-up Christmas tree, and off he'd go. The holidays always drag on, but without him the Yuletide season seemed interminable.

Sadly, the specter of AIDS provided a somber background to the 1980s. The virus was first identified in 1983, and by the late 1980s had become an epidemic. Thousands of young folks had died, mainly gay men, since it was transmittable through gay sex and unsterile drug paraphernalia. The first warning sign was usually the flu. Frederick suddenly came down with flu-like symptoms, and within a day was hospitalized at a small Culver

City Hospital. I trotted off to visit him with flowers and a silly teddy bear in hand, never imagining I'd be directed to the AIDS ward. There he was, sitting on a hospital bed connected to a few tubes. We just stared at each other for about twenty seconds, and then I fell apart. In those moments I was the victim and he was the stoic survivor. "Hey, I'm just HIV-positive. It's going to be okay. If and when I actually get AIDS, they'll have a cure," he reassured me. Oh, I believed it, because I wanted and *needed* to believe it.

A few days later, Frederick returned to his bungalow apartment, which was nicely decorated, but in a bad neighborhood. We both agreed that it wasn't safe, and that he should start looking for another place to live. After laboriously scouting around, we found a perfect loft-like condo in West Hollywood. Frederick adored it, but it was only for sale, not for rent. After some discussion, it was decided that we would bite the bullet and buy it. Between my mother, Frederick, and me, it was quickly arranged. Frederick would pay me $600 rent a month, with which I would pay the mortgage, the balance going to my mother. Our setup worked like a Swiss clock.

Frederick's white, somewhat modern furniture was perfect for the condo. Off-white drapes were ordered, and we filled the little patio with leafy plants and brightly colored flowers. Everything came together and looked stunning. Just a few large items had to be purchased, such as a refrigerator. All that mattered to Frederick was the exterior appearance. It had to be all white and smooth like satin, with no tiny little bumps, as was the fashion then. After a search—second only to the quest for the Holy Grail—we located one at a discount store. Great price, but non-returnable because it was a discontinued model.

With my dear friend, Frederick Combs.

After waiting days for delivery, Frederick's smooth, all-white refrigerator finally arrived. Unfortunately, not only did the door open the wrong way, but it was two inches too tall for the opening that Frederick had so carefully measured. (Shades of the air conditioner debacle.) After a week of climbing over and squeezing past this huge piece of useless metal, carpenters were summoned. They proceeded to destroy and rebuild the overhead cabinets while simultaneously trashing the kitchen floor.

Plumbers followed in their wake, and after a full day's labor put together parts of the discontinued ice maker that made one tray of smashed ice daily. Last, but not least, came the painters. The condo now had a small $1,000 used Frigidaire.

Finally, the condo was finished, and life returned to normal. Well, as normal as life could be with Frederick. I busied myself with my career, and he continued his teaching. His HIV symptoms rarely flared up. Life was good.

We often went to the beach, both of us loving the ocean. On several occasions, we drove up the coast for a weekend in Carpenteria, an artsy suburb just south of Santa Barbara. Friends of Frederick let us stay at their home when they were out of town.

The first weekend we went there, we dropped off our stuff, jumped into our bathing suits, and made a beeline for the local beach. After parking on Pacific Coast Highway, we walked down a steep incline to what appeared to be a semi-private beach. Whoa! Off to my right, a nude volleyball game was in progress. Men and women were leaping in the air, their uncovered body parts freely bobbing up and down. Well-endowed boobs were bouncing, men's private parts were bouncing, everything was bouncing! Ironically, one gal had on *something*, a baseball cap with her ponytail flying out the back. All in all, not a sight to behold. After catching my breath, I said, "Frederick, this is a nude beach. I don't do nude beaches."

"No, it's an anything goes beach. Come on, we'll go further down," he said with a laugh.

Finding a spot, we spread out our towels and lay down, soaking in the sun and beginning to relax. Out of nowhere, a beautiful, stark-naked woman, blond hair flowing in the breeze, passed in front of us. She was wearing only a Rolex watch and clutching a transistor radio attached to earphones.

Before I could pass a comment, Frederick said, "Let's go for a swim." We dove into the ocean and slowly freestyled through gentle waves toward the setting sun. The water was cool and calm. I went through my usual five-minute thing of seeing sharks everywhere, occasionally screaming out to Frederick, "Shark!"

He yelled back, "Stop it! Enough! There are no sharks."

The instant he said that, I looked over and saw what appeared to be a fin sticking out of the water and heading straight for me. I screamed even louder. "Shark!"

Frederick turned and saw what I saw, and yelled, "Swim!" We both went into high gear and churned frantically towards the shore like gold medal Olympic swimmers. All the time, we yelled back and forth to each other: "Keep going!" "Don't save me!" "Don't stir the water by kicking too hard!" "You can make it!"

At some point, I looked up and noticed a small group of people standing on the beach watching us. No one did anything or seemed to be in a panic; they were just taking in the action. As I neared the shore, the fin sticking out of the water raised its head. It was a friendly seal just wanting to say hello.

Relieved, but mortified by our farcically overwrought behavior, Frederick and I crept quietly and shamefacedly to our towels and lay back down. One or two onlookers empathized with our fear, but the others snickered and sneered as they walked away. City folks ruining their laid-back, somewhat-private beach.

Stretched out on our towels again, we'd just begun to relax, but were brought up short as a woman with two dogs and a spear in her hand ambled past us toward a pile of rocks farther out in the ocean, where she disrobed and proceeded to spear fish. Each time she nailed one, she would toss it back to the beach, where her canine companions would play with and guard the flopping fish. After a half hour or so, she returned to the beach, dressed, gathered her fish and her dogs, and headed back to her car. It was the end of a day at the beach for Frederick and me.

At dinner that night, I consumed more than my usual glass or two of wine before returning to the house for a well-earned sleep. Halfway through the night, I got cold and jumped into bed with Frederick. He muttered something like, "No cuddling," but the next morning we were wrapped around each other. So much for "no cuddling."

Later that Sunday, we headed back to Los Angeles. In what was to become a custom, we stopped for dinner at the Paradise Cove Beach Cafe just north of Malibu. It was filled with brightly costumed Hispanic people. Mariachis played lively songs, and folks were dancing. It was a Fiesta de Quinceañera, the celebration of a girl's coming of age at fifteen. We tried to not intrude on the celebration, but were soon drawn into the festivities. It was great fun and a lesson in Hispanic culture.

Frederick and I returned to Carpenteria several more times. Each trip was fun and relaxing, but nothing topped that first trip.

Around mid-1992, Frederick's health took a turn for the worse. His HIV diagnosis had become full-blown AIDS. For a while, we worked around it. I took care of his class finances and other matters, and a friend of his took over some of his classes. It wasn't long, though, before everything stopped and Frederick was confined to the condo with round-the-clock nurses. The Screen Actors Guild health plan was a godsend. I visited him almost every day. We would spend an hour or so watching television while I gave him a foot message, adjusted his pillows, and did what I could for him. I've never felt so helpless.

On September 19, 1992, Frederick passed away. Making his death more painful was the confused and inept handling of his estate. In some ways, it became a scene from *Zorba the Greek* (1964). His friend was the executor of his will, but Frederick left his personal belongings and everything in the condo to me, which did not sit well with the executor. However, that is not a story for this book. This book is titled *Hollywood With a Smile*, and that is the way Frederick would have wanted it.

JAMES "JIM" GARNER

1928–2014

How does one describe a bright, charming, handsome, witty con man? (The onscreen variety, of course.) If he's all of that and more, then he's James Garner.

(James Garner worked more than fifty different jobs and did a stint in the Marines, earning two Purple Hearts, before landing by chance a nonspeaking role in the 1954 Broadway production of The Caine Mutiny Court-Martial. *He learned his craft on the stage before moving on to commercials and television roles. He eventually landed a contract with Warner Bros, which led to a handful of films throughout the 1950s. In 1957, he starred in the hugely successful television series* Maverick *(1957–1962), in which he played a charming anti-hero gambler, until leaving over a contract dispute. He went on to star in such highly successful films as* The Great Escape *(1963),* The Americanization of Emily *(1964),* Grand Prix *(1966), and* Support Your Local Sheriff *(1969). Then came* The Rockford Files *(1974–1980), in which he again played a charismatic, against-the-grain hero. It was another highly successful television series, and won him an Emmy in 1974. The show ended due to Garner's knee and heart problems, as well as a conflict with Universal Studios over its creative accounting. He returned to films, notably* Victor Victoria *(1982) and* Murphy's Romance *(1985), as well as the big-screen version of* Maverick *(1996). He did several other television series, although none of them really took off. His last big success was the 2004 film* The Notebook.*)*

Java and Lunch with Jim

Every Sunday night, I would call my father in New York. This ritual began in the 1970s and continued until he passed away in the late 1980s. I would regale him with the follies and foibles of my week in Tinseltown, and he would patiently listen, occasionally interjecting an upbeat comment. At the end of our conversations, he would invariably say something like, "Sweetheart, think about being a stage actress. Come back to New York."

I would answer, "I'll think about it, Dad, but not until I've worked just once with James Garner. Remember when we used to watch *Maverick* together? You'd say, 'Now, there's a man I'd like to meet.' Well, I'm gonna meet him *for* you."

In 1974, it happened. I auditioned for and landed a nice role on the very first episode of *The Rockford Files*. I played a prim hostess at an upscale country club who succumbs to Jim's charm as he tries to gain entrance to a private outdoor patio. It was a fun scene in which Jim worked his charismatic magic to con me into showing him to a table. I was to become increasingly enamored as he charms me, casually removing my sweater to a reveal a tight red dress, then slipping off my glasses, then letting my hair come tumbling down. Finally, I would seductively say, "Come this way, Mr. Rockford. There's one empty table available."

Come the day of the shoot at the Bel-Air Country Club, I was anxiously pacing outside, going over my lines, trying to tie them together with the physical actions required, when a familiar voice behind me said, "Would you like to run lines with me?" Yeah, you got it. It was James Garner himself.

"I'd love that. Thank you!" I replied. "I'm a little nervous and trying to get the timing with the business right. Oh, I'm Sandy de Bruin, and I'm playing the hostess."

"Okay, then, Sandy de Bruin, let's go to work."

We proceeded to rehearse for the next few minutes, until the makeup man called me over to get freshened up prior to shooting the scene. Occupying the makeup chair was an attractive blond woman underneath a big straw hat. She was obviously one of the extras who would be seated on the patio. She didn't move when the makeup man politely asked her to please get out of his chair so he could touch me up. "Why? Who's *she*?" she asked, still seated. I glanced up, and saw Jim taking in her high and mighty attitude.

"She's the actress in the next scene with Mr. Garner, that's who she is," the makeup man responded with an edge in his voice. At that, she arrogantly stood up, slinked over to where Jim was standing, and tried to flirt with him. He gave her a blank look, muttered something or other, then turned and walked away.

Moments later, the scene was set. Jim and I were on our markers, and the extras were all seated on the patio. Just as were about to rehearse, Jim motioned the director over. In a quiet but firm voice, he said, "See that blond extra seated on the patio with the big straw hat? Lose her!"

The director called to the Assistant Director in charge of extras. Moments later, the woman was gone, but not before exchanging a few angry words with the AD. All I remember hearing was, "Just sign out. You'll be paid for the day."

I had never witnessed this kind of power, and was quite taken aback. Jim, the total professional, just calmly turned to me and said, "Let's do it." We did, and the take came off without a hitch.

Unfortunately, when the episode aired, the hair-tumbling-down part was cut. But the scene was impressive enough to be used in previews and PR blurbs for *The Rockford Files.*

When filming was over, I said thanks to everyone on the set, drove home, and immediately called my father. This time, he didn't end our talk with the usual, "Come home, sweetheart." He knew I was hooked—and thriving—in Hollywood.

After a year or so, I was again cast in *The Rockford Files*, this time playing a nurse at the Malibu hospital where Rockford was taken whenever he needed medical help. My first scene was simply assisting the doctor in removing buckshot from Rockford's butt. Jim hated the scene and was in no mood for any mishaps, so the set was tense from the start. It definitely wasn't timely for me to reintroduce myself. However, we got through it okay.

The next scene had me running through the hospital entrance, then skidding to a halt and screaming, "It's Rockford, and he's been shot!" (Films and television shows are rarely filmed in sequence, so while this scene took place prior to the buckshot scene, it was actually done afterward.)

There was no rehearsal, as it was a fairly simple shot. I ran through the entrance and yelled my line in my inimitable fashion. I then heard the dreaded words: "Cut! You missed the marker, Sandy. Let's do it again." Jim, seated in his chair watching the action, loudly muttered, "Jesus Christ, she can't even hit the marker."

Looking down in vain for a marker, I instantly responded, "Sorry, I'll get it right next time."

Suddenly, an angry voice rang down from the rafters: "There *is* no marker!"

Dead silence.

Apparently, this crew member had had enough of Jim's attitude for the day. Within minutes, a marker was set down on the floor, and I nailed the scene in one take.

Right after that, lunch was called. I retreated to my trailer, hoping to avoid any further encounters. A few minutes later, there was a knock on my door. I hesitantly opened it. Standing below me was Jim. He studied me for a moment before asking, "Why didn't you say there was no marker?"

I paused, then hesitantly replied, "They're your crew. I'm only here for the day."

He knew what I meant, but didn't respond directly. He just said, "Get some lunch. We've got good caterers," and walked away.

I had one more scene that day, but it wasn't with Jim. I just had to shuffle some paper at the nurse's station and murmur a few remarks. When I returned to my trailer, I was greeted by a lovely, understated bouquet of spring flowers and a card that read, simply, yet meaningfully, "James Garner."

A few weeks or a month passed. One day, my agent called with exciting news: *The Rockford Files* wanted me to reappear as the Malibu Nurse. It was just a one-day part, but it came with a raise. Thus began my first recurring role on a television show.

My scene this time as the Malibu Nurse (they never gave me a name) was at the same nurse station looking through some files when Rockford enters and asks for the room number of a friend he's come to visit. I greet him and give him the number. A subsequent scene was a reverse of the first: Rockford leaving the hospital and saying goodbye to me. Both scenes were scheduled for after the lunch break, but my call was earlier, so I'd be ready after lunch.

After being fitted in wardrobe and made up, I filled my lunch tray and found a seat off by myself. I had a slight lingering unease from the marker incident during my last appearance on the show, and thought it best to maintain a respectful distance from everyone. As I sat down, a voice behind me asked, "May I join you?" It was Jim. Tray in hand, he promptly sat down with me. Somehow, there was no gulf between star and aspiring actress, a testament to his fundamentally down-to-earth nature. We proceeded to have a cordial and interesting conversation about everything except the show. His career, my career. His likes and dislikes. He even touched on his current knee problems. Feeling relaxed in his presence, I couldn't resist reminding him that we had worked together before on the first episode of his hit series. He looked at me blankly, the wheels obviously turning.

"I played the hostess at the country club," I reminded him.

A pause, then a smile. "Ah, yes, now I remember. You did a good job. Sorry I didn't remember you, but it's a bit of a visual stretch from upscale hostess to ER nurse."

"Yeah, it is, and you work with so many actors, you can't be expected to remember them all. But it was such a thrill to be working that day, much less on a one-on-one scene with you. I was a nervous wreck."

"I'm always nervous whenever I work. Don't let it get to you. Just go out there and do the job," he said.

Right about then it was time to get back to work. We soon finished for the day, and home I went. Glowing. Like a full moon.

I played the Malibu Nurse two or three more times, often opposite Jim. Other times, I would run into him on set, and we would have coffee and chat. My favorite encounter with him on *The Rockford Files* occurred near the end of the series.

James Garner at the 39th
Emmy Awards, 1987.

There I am: the Malibu Nurse. This time we were shooting on a sound stage at Universal Studios. Another scene was being shot, and I was just standing around when the assistant director approached me and said, "Security wants to see you at the sound stage entrance." I was somewhat mystified as he led the way. There, standing beside the security guard, was Damian, the quintessential ten-year old Tom Sawyer, who had been living with me in my tiny apartment for the past few months.

The guard looked at Damian, then at me. "He says he's your son and was looking for you. Somehow or other he got onto the lot, where I caught him. Then I tracked you down through the casting office."

"Oh, thank you. I'm sorry if he caused any trouble," was all I could say.

"Next time, leave him a pass," the guard said as he walked away.

I hugged Damian and told him we'd discuss this later, but in the meantime to just come with me and be quiet. Back at the set, we both stood silently until Damian got restless and inquisitive and started asking questions. Why was that person holding a pole? What were the lights for? What was that guy doing on an extension ladder with a camera?

"I can't leave right now," I told him. "Hold on for a moment and let me see if I can find somebody important to show you around."

From behind us I heard, "Will I do?" You guessed it. Jim.

I laughed. "Don't think we can do better!"

Introductions and "nice to meet you" greetings were quickly dispensed, then Jim graciously asked Damian what he would most like to see.

"That guy on the big ladder with the camera."

Jim immediately took Damian to meet "that guy on the ladder with a camera." Damian was soon sitting next to the cameraman, having the thrill of his life.

Jim strolled back over to me. Did I discern a gleam in his eye? "I thought you told me you didn't have any children."

"I don't," I responded. "But I sort of do now. He's a neighborhood kid whose bicycle I rescued, and as a result we became friends. A few months ago, his mother dropped him off at my bungalow to stay for a long weekend, and she's never returned. Once in a while she phones in, but that's it."

"You're kidding," Jim replied.

"No, but it's okay. He's the kind of kid I've always wanted, and he and his dog, Higgins, and my dog, Nada, all get along great. It works! But school is looming, and the bureaucratic powers that be might get Social Services involved. That's gonna be a problem."

Before Jim could reply, Damian returned, and Jim, bless him, focused all his attention on my almost-son. Jim took him all around the set, answered all of Damian's questions, then left him at the Honey Wagon food truck with instructions to the cook to give the boy whatever his heart desired.

Right about then, I did my Malibu Nurse scene. Once we wrapped, I gave profuse and heartfelt thanks to Jim, said my goodbyes to everyone else, grabbed Damian, and headed for my car. On the way home, I suggested that after we picked the dogs up, we should all go to our favorite drive-in for dinner. Hamburgers for everyone, but no onions for the dogs!

"Don't need to. I got enough food at the Honey Wagon for dinner," Damian proudly said, reaching into his pockets and producing an astonishing array of Honey Wagon goodies. Looking down in horror at Damian's booty, I thought, *Oh, God, this might just be my last* Rockford Files. It was, but only because the show was canceled in 1980 due to Universal's questionable accounting. (Jim and his production company, Cherokee, took the studio to court, and eventually won.)

A year went by, and then Jim got back in the saddle in *Bret Maverick* (1981–1982), reprising the role he played in the original series. I was called in to audition for a screaming, hysterical woman on an episode of the remake. After howling like a madwoman and muttering incoherently, I walked out of the casting office, and smack into Jim. We happily greeted each other, and then he asked, in some astonishment, "Was that *you* they had auditioning for the screaming woman?"

"Yeah," I answered.

"What?" he snapped, with that glazed expression on his face, the one I recognized that meant someone was going to hear about this.

The first of my five appearances
on *The Rockford Files* (1974).

"It's okay, Jim. I need the job. Let it go," I said, trying to calm him down.

"I don't think so," he responded, and proceeded to storm into the casting office.

Of course, I got the role.

A few weeks later, it was announced that *Bret Maverick* had been picked up for another season. My agent called to tell me I had been offered a recurring role as a saloon girl at the Red Ox Saloon. The producers were guaranteeing me six out of twelve shows, which meant I would be doing at least six shows, and possibly twelve. After catching my breath and yelling out the window, I asked, "How did this happen? I never auditioned for a saloon girl, but, God, that would be a dream come true."

"Oh, it's the same producers from *The Rockford Files*. They know you, and apparently Jim likes you. Also, it says on your resume that you're a dancer, which probably gave you another edge up. They're sending over the contracts. I'll get back to you when they arrive."

The contracts duly arrived, and after a bit of back and forth with the producers, a contract was signed by one and all. Everyone, especially me, was deliriously happy.

As often happens in Hollywood, however, seemingly done deals can evaporate in a heartbeat. A week or so after my contract was sealed, the network announced that it was canceling *Bret Maverick*, and all contracts were therefore null and void. There are no words to describe my disappointment, which was followed by weeks of depression. Fortunately, roles on other shows kept the bills paid and me from slitting my wrists.

Jim by now had had enough of television and the networks, and went on to do some of the most remarkable films of his career, including *Victor Victoria* (1982) and *Murphy's Romance* (1985). Unfortunately, being known primarily as a television actor, I wasn't considered for roles in these films.

In 1991, Jim headlined another television series, *Man of the People* (1991–1992), in which he played a small-town councilman. He still had that charming con-man aura, a man that didn't play by the rules. A few shows into production, I successfully auditioned for the role of Shirley, the proverbial hooker with a heart of gold. (I had played a similar character on other shows.) Mine was a simple jail scene in which Jim's character is there to bail out an incarcerated friend when he notices me behind bars.

The director was setting up the scene, with me dressed like a trashy call girl, when I spotted Jim seated in his personalized chair watching the rehearsal. "Hi, Jim," I called out. "I'm back again, only this time I'm in jail."

He laughed. "Recognized the voice, but not the outfit."

Jim's part called for him to walk past my jail cell, recognize me, stop, and say, "Hey, Shirley, how's it going?"

"Ahh, after 40, it's all panache," I reply good-naturedly, while freshening my breath with mouth spray. "But right now, I could do with a little influence."

"I'll see what I can do," he responds.

"Do that and you get a freebie!" I yell back.

After the second rehearsal, the director called out: "Jim, step in closer. You're out of the shot."

"No," Jim answered. "It's her scene. Give *her* the shot." So it was.

Afterwards, as was our custom, Jim and I had a quick coffee together and nattered until his next scene came up. I bid him goodbye, feeling really good about the work we'd done.

A few days later, my agent rang me, not bothering to conceal his excitement. "*Man of the People* wants you to come back as Jim's regular hooker! There's no contract yet, but it looks good."

Again, euphoria and celebrations. Shades of *Bret Maverick*, though, a week later, the network canceled *Man of the People*. Another case of almost but not quite, and my one chance to snuggle with James Garner was gone.

I never had the good fortune to work with Jim again. I followed his career as he went on to do more noteworthy films such as *My Fellow Americans* (1996) and *The Notebook* (2004). Every year, until his passing in 2014, I sent him a Christmas card. I always signed under my name: The Malibu Nurse. More often than not, I would get one in return.

There were few actors—or men, for that matter—as talented, charming, kind, and strong as James Garner. He wasn't afraid to stand up for himself or for others when he felt that something was wrong or unfair. Thank you, Jim, for being you in my dreams, and being just you in real life.

CHARLTON "CHUCK" HESTON

1923–2008

Heroic men in films always stand out. They often portray real-life heroes from the past. Some even play God and become legends. Charlton Heston was just such a film icon, but so much more than that.

(Charlton Heston was more than an unforgettable film star. He was also a Civil Rights activist who supported Martin Luther King in the 1960s, and was always involved in politics working for what he personally believed in, no matter what political parties were involved or how controversial they were. This 6'3," ruggedly handsome man was born in Illinois in 1923 to a middle-class family. He began acting on stage and performed in regional theaters throughout his fifty-year Hollywood tenure. His career followed the usual arc: small films, stage productions, etc. His breakthrough to stardom came in 1956 when he starred in the film The Ten Commandments. *He followed that in 1959 with* Ben-Hur, *winning a well-deserved Academy Award for best actor. Then came* El Cid *(1961), another historical blockbuster.* The Agony and the Ecstasy *(1965) was more or less the end of his portrayals of past heroes and icons. He branched out and did eclectic films such as* Planet of the Apes *(1968),* Call of the Wild *(1972),* Soylent Green *(1973), and a few disaster films. As time went on, he became more involved in politics. He was president of the Screen Actors' Guild from 1966–1971 and president of the controversial National Rifle Association in the 1990s, but still*

managed to dabble in television and stage work. Throughout his journey through the film industry he kept journals and wrote. His last book was In the Arena *(1995), in which he celebrates his blessings.)*

Work and Wine with Chuck

In the mid-1980s, a collection of high-profile stars, as well as lesser-known working actors like me, formed a group called Actors Working for an Actors Guild (AWAG). Its goal was to keep the Screen Actors Guild (SAG) exclusive for film actors and not open it up to other performing artists, all of whom had their own unions, but wanted to become a part of SAG, which offered more benefits and more power. Unfortunately, we were often labeled "elitists." SAG was intent on including all other entertainment unions under its umbrella, and it was becoming somewhat of a two-party political struggle. AWAG was headed up by Charlton Heston, known for throwing himself into political causes he personally believed in.

At the time, I was co-chairing the successful SAG Agents Relations Committee with the well-respected actor Don Dubbins. Don was my friend (and a personal friend of Heston's), and was also heavily involved with AWAG. He insisted I join him for the first general meeting to be held at a banquet hall somewhere in the San Fernando Valley. Off we went.

There were about 100 people in the hall. In the front of the room on a dais were Don, the famed actress Marie Windsor, Chuck, and several less-prominent actors. Chuck explained what AWAG was about and then took questions from the floor. Something came up about a legal precedent dating back to when SAG first became a guild. I raised my hand. Chuck motioned to me and said, "You?"

"Isn't there a statute of limitation on that?" I replied.

He looked at me—or I should say through me—and asked, "Why do you say that?"

"Because there seems to be a statute of limitation on almost everything except murder, kidnapping, and international espionage. If such a statute applies, then the problem is solved."

That clicked in his head, and I now had his full attention. "Are you a lawyer? What's your name?"

"I'm Sandra de Bruin, and, no, I'm not a lawyer."

"Thank you, Sandra. Good point, and we'll check into it." He turned his attention to other questions. As it turned out, there was no statute of limitation on the issue, but it was worth looking into.

While driving me home after the meeting, Don said that Chuck had invited me to the next closed informal meeting. "You impressed the big fellow," he said with a laugh.

Don played chauffeur to me for the next gathering a week later in an office building, also situated in the Valley. We sat down at a craft table with Chuck at the head, along with three men and a woman named Renee, with whom I'd had several bad encounters at SAG meetings. Following introductions, a visibly angry Renee demanded, "What is *she* doing here?" Obviously not one of my fans, nor happy to see me.

"I invited her," Chuck responded.

"Well, maybe she could take notes. That would be useful," was Renee's sarcastic reply.

A stunned silence followed, as everyone registered her apparent dislike for me. Before anyone could react, I spoke up. "I'd be happy to. I need a pen and some paper."

Without a moment's hesitation, Chuck slid his gold-plated pen down the table to me and said, "Here, use mine. Somebody get Sandra some paper."

I proceeded to take copious notes throughout the meeting. When we wrapped up, I handed Chuck back his pen. He said, "Drop the notes off at my house when you're done. It's off of Coldwater Canyon just south of Mulholland. The gates are always open, and it has a long driveway."

I typed up the notes that evening with the professional polish I'd learned while moonlighting as a secretary early in my Hollywood career, then drove to Chuck's house the next day. After navigating the long driveway to the front of the house, I was greeted by three large mature dogs, all anxious to see who this intruder was. I love dogs, but these seemed a bit intimidating, so I remained seated behind the wheel. Just as I was about to honk for help, an elderly man shuffled up to my car and said, "It's okay, miss. Just get out. It's their way of greeting people."

I exited with some hesitation, petted the dogs without incident, walked to the front door, and rang the bell. This was opened by yet another elderly person, a woman. I explained who I was and why I was there. She asked me to wait. A few moments later, a lovely, well-dressed, middle-aged woman appeared. It was Carol Lanning, Chuck's personal assistant and secretary. I handed her my AWAG notes, and after a brief but cordial chat went on my way. I didn't realize it at the time, but this was the start of a delightful personal and professional relationship. Carol had worked for Mr. Heston (as she always called him) for many years, and continued to work for him until his passing. In fact, all of his employees were extremely loyal and remained at their jobs forever, a tribute to both Mr. and Mrs. Heston.

Actor Charlton Heston, American
Film Institute president, 1981.

Chuck called that evening. Extremely pleased with my notes, he asked if I would like to be the official AWAG secretary. No salary, but all expenses paid. Of course, I jumped at the chance. A week or so later, I was invited to a meeting/cocktail party at Marie Windsor's home. Over several glasses of wine, Chuck and Marie brought me up to date on past AWAG happenings. It was a great way to start a job (albeit non-paying), surrounded by celebrities, chatting with Charlton Heston, and sipping fantastic wine.

Unfortunately, the other unofficial board members were not as enthusiastic about me. Chuck usually saw things as black or white, but I could often make him see the gray, and then he would cut back the PR rhetoric. This infuriated them. They felt threatened by the perception that I had Chuck's ear. As time went by, they made my life quite difficult—misrepresenting me, signing my name to documents, accusing me of having too close a relationship with SAG's National Executive Director, Ken Orsatti, etc. Most of that stopped after I angrily brought the last incident to Carol's attention. I never did find out who put a stop to it, she or Chuck. I thought it best not to ask or dwell on it and let sleeping dogs lie. My forged signature never appeared on a document again.

Carol and I subsequently became friends. We occasionally met after she was through with work for dinner in West Los Angeles, or we'd have coffee at Chuck's house. She once gave me a grand tour of the Heston estate. Chuck and Lydia, his wife, who enjoyed photography, had separate work spaces, but the rest of the house was filled with memorabilia from Chuck's films and family photos. Nope, no chariot!

As the weeks went by, I learned that part of Chuck's success was due to his strong philosophy of don't talk the talk, walk the walk. When one wants or believes in something, go for it and go for it now. If Chuck had something on his mind or wanted to discuss something, he was instantly on the phone to me, day or night. I think he enjoyed talking with me. It gave him a perspective on those of us "down here on the ground," to quote the character Che in Broadway's *Evita* (1979). Like many celebrities who soon forget their earlier struggles, he appreciated being reminded. When it was brought to his attention that one of our unofficial board members was doing gay porno films, Chuck simply replied, "Well, at least he's working." What an open-minded remark from a man often labeled by the press as a right-wing fanatic because of his support for Ronald Reagan and his involvement with the National Rifle Association.

Answering services were widely popular from the 1960s to 1990s, and are still in use today. Like having a personal secretary, they can give you a wake-up call in the morning or forward important calls, like from your agent, to wherever you happen to be. (The 1960 movie *Bells Are Ringing*, starring Judy Holliday and Dean Martin, fancifully centered on the personal possibilities of the answering service.)

I was at a friend's house in Bel Air one afternoon when the phone rang. She answered it, and immediately went into shock. Covering the receiver with her hand, she whispered, "*Charlton Heston* wants to speak to you."

I grabbed the phone and said, "Hi, Chuck," further discombobulating my friend. After a quick conversation, it was decided that I would meet him in an hour in the back room at the Beverly Glen Center off Mulholland Drive. This was more or less a "celebrity" location not patronized by the public. When I arrived, Chuck stood up to greet me (always the gentleman). We talked some business, had a few glasses of wine, and chatted and laughed like old friends. That late-afternoon meeting, sitting there with Moses, or better yet, Ben-Hur, is one of my fondest show business memories.

One of my last personal encounters with Chuck took place on a warm California spring day. I had driven to his home with some bad news about AWAG. Headlining *The Hollywood Reporter* was an article calling AWAG a group of elitists (again!), citing the fact that many of our members were stepping back from it. Upon arriving, I was directed to the tennis court, where an informal game was going on. Chuck, dressed in tennis attire but not part of the game, immediately acknowledged me and waved me towards him. I started to tell him about the headline, but he already knew. (He was always a step ahead of me.) Then he said, "Do you play tennis?"

"Yeah. Well, I should say, I play *at* tennis, since I only play doubles."

"Well, then, let's play."

"I don't think that's a good idea."

"Why not?"

"Because you don't like to lose, and with me playing, we'll lose."

He chuckled and said, "You're getting to know me." With that, he motioned to someone to bring us a glass of wine. I stayed for another half hour and then drove home, knowing that AWAG was about to go down in spite of Chuck's efforts for what I still believe was the right call.

A few weeks after our almost tennis game, SAG members, backed by the Teamsters Union, voted to include extras under their umbrella. They won the war, and AWAG dissolved. Since then, AFTRA and all other performing unions have become a part of SAG. The members of our unofficial board went their separate ways. Only a few of us continued our acting careers.

I kept in touch with Chuck for years, mainly through his assistant, Carol Lanning. He warmly signed his books for me and even signed the script of *Gray Lady Down* (1978), in which I had a (very) small part. The story was about a sinking submarine, so the entire cast was male, with only two credited female roles: wives with one line each.

The last time I saw Chuck was in 2007 at Art's Deli in Studio City. He was paying his bill at the counter when I ran over to greet him, only to be held back by two young men. Somewhat startled, I called, "Chuck! It's me, Sandra."

He looked up and motioned me forward. It was then that I noticed how frail he looked. He smiled and stroked my hand, asking the usual polite questions. "How are you? How is your career going?" I blew him a kiss as he left, but he didn't turn back.

I spoke with Carol shortly afterward. She told me that Chuck was indeed ill with Alzheimer's. The trip to Art's Deli was one of his last outings. Soon after, the press was notified that Charlton Heston was withdrawing from public life. Electronic gates were installed at the front of his driveway, and he never made another public appearance. He passed away in 2008. I was not invited to his memorial service, but I was okay with that. It was a private affair, the way he would have wanted it.

Why would an icon with such incredible mental acumen, loyalty, passion, and physical attributes have to suffer such a horrendous end of life? I can only fall back on the Bob Dylan song. "The answer, my friend, is blowing in the wind. The answer is blowing in the wind."

C. BERNARD "JACK" JACKSON

1927–1996

The man, his mission, his music. A man that had it all, did it all, and made it count.

(C. Bernard Jackson, known to all as "Jack," first became a recognizable figure in the arts world when in 1962 he won an Obie Award (the awards for off-Broadway plays) for his musical play Fly Blackbird. *Soon after the Watts riots in 1965, he took over a former Masonic temple in Los Angeles, which quickly became the Inner City Cultural Center (ICCC). It was an arts oasis and sanctuary for underprivileged youth, and a stage for ethnic performers. It nurtured the careers of such artists as Beah Richards, George Takei, Forest Whitaker, and Edward James Olmos, among others. Jack was an outspoken speaker for the arts and for multicultural diversity. He spent thirty years as executive director of ICCC, and was often interviewed by the press and on television. Along the way, Jack was appointed a member of the Kennedy Arts Council in Washington D.C. and a member of the Board of the California Arts Council. His numerous honors include the Dramalogue award, the* LA Weekly *award, and the NAACP Trailblazer and Image awards. His newsworthy quote, "Art may be the only tool we have left to save ourselves from destruction" is still relevant today.)*

My Friend Jack:
Unforgettable in Every Way

Jack was probably the brightest light in my life, as well as thousands of other lives. His quiet persistence in everything that he did made him a Los Angeles icon from the mid-1960s through the 1990s. But I'm getting ahead of myself.

Jack first came into my life in 1960, when I was 19 years old. At that time, I was a part-time secretary/receptionist in the dance department at UCLA, so naturally I took that opportunity to take free dance classes. Jack played the bongo drums during these sessions to pay tuition for his master's degree in music. Since he was most often late for his classes, the head of the dance department, Alma Hawkins, asked me to give him a morning wake-up call whenever he was scheduled to play. As the years went by, I realized punctuality was a minor flaw in Jack's character. The world had one time, and Jack had another! My wake-up calls became a fun routine, wherein Jack and I often bantered about life, the arts, and coffee.

One morning, Alma asked me to remind Jack that the press was going to be covering her class and to tell him in my morning wake-up call to wear a jacket. He replied, "I only have one, but okay." He arrived with a wrinkled K-Mart jacket and a white shirt with missing buttons. I quickly pulled him together as best I could, telling him to leave the jacket with me and I'd sew a button on it. Then off we went to our morning dance class.

During class, we often locked eyes. There was such an attraction! Jack was a good-looking, light-skinned Black man about 5'10", lean with sharp features and an easy smile. Now that I think about it, the way he walked with that casual, easy stride reminds me of Barack Obama. In his later years, he grew a beard, which made him even more dashing.

After dance class, Jack casually approached me. "Wanna go to lunch?" he asked. He added sarcastically, "We can picnic outside on the perfectly groomed UCLA lawn." Which we did. That was the start of a liaison that lasted thirty-five years.

We did picnic lunches for a few short months and talked about everything. One day, he told me that the musical play he had written and would be directing, *Fly Blackbird*, had been accepted at an off-Broadway theatre in New York City, and that he would be leaving soon. My heart sank. Before I could comment, he said, "Come with me." For a moment, I thought he was kidding, but then realized he meant it.

Stunned by his offer, I reminded him I was newly married to a med student and that such a thing was impossible and unacceptable.

He quickly echoed, "Unacceptable? In what way? Is it because I'm Black, or because I'm a musical playwright/artist, or because being married to a doctor is what's expected of you?"

I tearfully explained to him that it had nothing to do with him being Black or an artist, but I could not leave the man I had just married and thought I loved, not to mention upending my socially status-conscious New York family.

He empathically countered, "You'll never make it as a doctor's wife. It's not in you. You're part of the arts, not a doctor's housewife." (He was right. The marriage didn't last, and soon I went on to a fairly successful acting career.) Jack's last words on the subject were, "The offer stands. Think about it."

A week later, Jack took off for The Big Apple. *Fly Blackbird* was a tremendous hit, and won an Obie Award. It was the first all-Black play to receive such an award. Yeah, he was on his way to becoming the man of the hour. Well, the Black man of the hour. As the years passed, I occasionally read about Jack's many diverse accomplishments.

In 1970, I lucked out and was cast in a small part as a cowardly technician in the successful sci-fi movie *The Andromeda Strain,* directed and produced by Robert Wise, a four-time Academy Award winner. It was released with great fanfare in 1971; the premiere was at The Pantages Theatre in Hollywood. I couldn't believe it: I was invited. The invitation announced it as a benefit for the Inner City Cultural Center, but I didn't make the connection to Jack because I was so excited at being formally invited. The only thing on my mind was what to wear to such a gala.

The big night arrived. Simply but elegantly dressed, I drove my little red convertible to the front of the theatre, where a parking valet checked my ID and gave me a parking stub before driving it off to be parked with the swanky limousines. It looked so cute, all red and shiny nestled between Hollywood's most elegant vehicles.

The Pantages lobby was crowded with nicely dressed folks with unfamiliar faces. I wasn't quite sure what to do next. Suddenly, I felt someone take my arm, and a voice said, "Glad you could make it. You look lovely, Sandra, quite different from the green uniform you wore in the film. Can I get you a glass of wine?" It was Robert Wise.

After the usual social amenities, we headed to the bar. Before we reached it, a voice from behind us yelled, "Mr. Wise!" We both turned around to identify its owner. It was Jack. Before Bob could even acknowledge him, I yelled, "Jack!" Jack yelled, "de Bruin!" and we fell into each other's arms. It had been over ten years since we had seen each other or even been in contact. That didn't matter. It was as if it was only yesterday that we were picnicking on the UCLA lawn.

Un-entwining ourselves, we turned back to Bob, who stood, arms crossed, absorbing our reunion. Smiling, he said, "Obviously, you two know each other."

"Yes," I gleefully responded. "He played the bongo drums for my dance class at UCLA."

Bob chuckled. "Well, he's certainly come a long way since playing the bongo drums. Now he's the man of the hour, the Artistic Director and Founder of the Inner City Cultural Center, something Los Angeles certainly needed and can be very proud of. We honor it and him tonight," he said in that rather formal way he spoke.

At that moment, everything clicked in. Jack *was* the Inner City Cultural Center. How could I have been so oblivious and self-absorbed not to have realized it when I read the invitation?

"Thank you," Jack humbly responded. The two of them exchanged greetings and warmly shook hands.

However, we all realized the fund-raising premiere had to be a success and it was important that both men circulate. Before going our separate ways, Jack pulled out a pad of paper and a pen. I quickly wrote down my phone number, signed it with a heart, and handed it back. We all disappeared into the crowd, watched *The Andromeda Strain*, and went home.

Late that night, my phone rang. It was Jack. Two days later, we were having dinner at Jack's favorite place, the Dresden Restaurant on Vermont, a far cry from picnics on the UCLA lawn. We talked about our careers, our loves, and the past ten years. He now spoke several languages, had traveled to Africa (where he

C. Bernard Jackson, the best of men.

learned Swahili), and was a frequent honorary guest speaker throughout the United States. But he was proudest of the ICCC, which was located in what he cheerfully called "gangland." It was a creative sanctuary for kids, keeping them off the streets and out of jail. Jack was at the top of his game. Hours later, we returned to my place. It was the start of an on-again, off-again twenty-year romance.

In spite of our mutual attraction, my career, and Jack's dedication to the ICCC weren't conducive to a committed relationship. I would often drop by the center or the Ivar Theatre in Hollywood, which was now (actually had been for some time) attached to the ICCC. I'd help out or attend productions. Jack's staff was always friendly and accepting of me. He would attend my plays, gatherings, and parties, and watch my TV shows when he could. Occasionally, we would squeeze in a leisurely evening or weekend. We would often join friends for dinner and a film or a board game during the next few years. We would go our separate ways, and then suddenly be together again. In between, I would get involved with other men, and he would date other women. We never questioned each other about our personal affairs, we just accepted them. One day, while visiting the ICCC, Jack introduced me to a beautiful, multitalented Black actress named Emily Yancy. What an incredible lady. It was obvious to me that this was someone really special to Jack. Quite naturally at this point, our romantic involvement changed to one of deep friendship.

A month or so later was Jack's birthday, so I invited him and Emily to Cirque du Soleil at the beach. It was a beautiful clear Southern California night. The stars were bright, with the surf crashing in the background: a picture postcard. Jack was enthralled with it all, especially the show. Never before had I seen him so excited. Afterward, Jack suggested we go for a drink at a jazz club he knew in South Los Angeles. It was his birthday, so the sky was the limit. We drove to the club, got out of our car, and headed for the door, but before we could enter, a huge man, obviously a bouncer, stepped in front of Jack. Pointing at me, he said, "This is a Black club, no Whites allowed."

Taken aback, Jack responded, "What? She's with us!"

"I don't care if she's with Jesus Christ. She's White, and this is a Black-only club."

Jack shuffled his feet and looked up at the bouncer. In a controlled, icy voice, he replied, "Hey, brother, this is L.A., where *everyone* is welcome."

"Man, I don't make the rules. I just work here," the bouncer responded.

At this point, Emily jumped in. "Don't make a scene, Jack. Let's go! I know another club where we *all* will be welcome." I started to reach for Jack to drag him away, but Emily stopped me. "Stay out of it. This might be about you, but it's not your fight."

After a few more exchanges with the bouncer, we collected ourselves and went to another jazz club where my skin color wasn't a problem. Drinks flowed freely. Somehow or other, well after midnight, we all arrived safely at our appropriate homes.

Not long after that evening, I landed a *Secret* deodorant ad. It was a national commercial, which is every actor's dream, as its residual payout can buy one a house in Beverly Hills. I excitedly called Jack to tell him the news. He immediately said, "Yes! Meet me tonight at the Dresden Room, and we'll celebrate."

Emily joined us soon after I arrived. After ordering drinks, Jack raised his glass and said, "To the Black and White versions of a *Secret* commercial." Yep, you got it! Emily had booked the Black version of the same *Secret* commercial as I had. Another great evening of laughing, drinking, and celebrating ensued.

Alas, my elation was short-lived. When my theatrical agency heard about my booking a *Secret* commercial, it was pointed out that my contract with the agency clearly stated that I was forbidden to do any feminine hygiene commercials. (What can I say? It was a different era.) In their minds, a deodorant commercial fell into that category. I was devastated, but not more so than my commercial agent, who tried in vain to have my theatrical agent reconsider. To no avail.

A few more years passed, and my deep friendship with Jack continued. He would invite me to the ICCC to judge the finals for their acting classes. He, of course, would write the script, and I, of course, could not read it because he had scribbled all over the copy making last-minute changes. Round and round we would go, finally ending up with a mutually agreed-upon presentation. Other times, we would just hang out together at local pubs in the area.

In late April of 1992, my mother passed away, and I went back to New York City to take care of family matters. Just after leaving Los Angeles, the infamous 1992 riots, looting and civil disturbances erupted in South Central Los Angeles, sparked by the Rodney King police exonerations. The unrest quickly moved north closer to where I lived in the Larchmont area. Thousands of federal troops were called in for riot control. It was horrendous watching it on the news from New York. When I returned home in early May, things had settled down, but the city was still angry. Black men were being perceived by the unenlightened as the enemy.

A few days after I returned, Jack and I started spending a lot of time together at my house. Emily and he now had a platonic relationship. Jack would saunter off to the ICCC in the mornings and usually, but not always, return to see me in the evenings. One night when he wasn't there, I was awakened by my two dogs barking hysterically at the driveway where I parked my car. I saw nothing unusual when I looked out the living room window, and went back to bed. The next morning, I went out to my car and noticed that my umbrella and a few other things I kept in it were lying on the ground. Then I saw it. The entire car interior looked like a melted blackened marshmallow. It had been packed full of newspaper and set on fire. It was totaled. According to the fire department, I was lucky that the car windows and sunroof had been tightly closed. Otherwise, the flames would have escaped and probably set my house on fire.

I called Jack, in hysterics. After hearing what happened, he promised to come by later. He wasn't particularly sympathetic, just very, very angry. That evening, after a couple of drinks, Jack quietly said, "I have to go, and I won't be back."

I was stunned. "Why? What are you talking about?"

"Obviously, your neighbors or someone either hates Blacks or is blaming the Blacks for the riots. Who knows? But my being here is too dangerous for you."

"It can't be because you are staying here. Maybe it was just arbitrary. Or maybe someone really hates me," I argued.

It was no use. A short time later, Jack gathered up the few things he had lying around the house, hugged me, and left.

Time went on, as it has a way of doing. Jack and I kept in close touch and often saw each other, but almost always in public. The ICCC was still thriving, but the building was decaying, partly from damage incurred by the 1992 riots. Unfortunately, Jack's financial acumen didn't match his charisma and artistic talent, and finances through grants were on the decline.

In 1994, the terrible Northridge earthquake struck. The entire Los Angeles area was horrifically affected. Many people were killed, and thousands were injured. Among the countless buildings severely damaged or collapsed was the ICCC. The building was condemned. Jack was devastated. He tried to pull it together again, but there was no money to be found. Getting a loan was impossible, as he had no collateral. He managed to hang on to the Ivar Theater in Hollywood, and often presented plays and competitions there. But it wasn't the same. Nothing was the same. Soon, his health started to decline and his drinking began to escalate.

In the summer of 1995, I moved to Denver. I thought I'd be a big fish in a little pond. Alas, there was no pond. Although I signed with the city's top agent, nothing worked out. Throughout my months there, Jack and I kept in touch via phone calls.

I'd tell him how miserable I was, and he'd say, "Come on home, de Bruin. Things are starting to happen. I've written a play again. You'll love it. I miss you."

So, in the late spring of 1996, as soon as the snow melted over the Rockies, less than ten months after having arrived in Denver, I arranged for a mover, loaded up my car with my two dogs and a few personal belongings, and headed back to my new home in Studio City in the Golden State, never to leave again.

The day after arriving home, Jack called, very excited. His new play was opening that night with great fanfare at the Music Center Annex in downtown Los Angeles, twenty miles from Studio City. He had reserved an orchestra seat for me. As pleased and happy as I was for him, I told him I was still just too exhausted from the drive to attend. Adding to that, my furniture hadn't arrived, I was sleeping on the floor, and my two dogs were disoriented and acting out.

"Come on, you can make it. You'll love the show," he begged.

"I'm sure I would, but as much as my heart and soul would love to be there, I just physically can't," I said.

"Well, I'm going to hold your seat in the hope you change your mind."

"Don't think so, Jack, but I'll be thinking good thoughts, and I love you." That ended the conversation. Much to my regret, I didn't attend. The play was a hit, and the reviews the next day were terrific.

I talked to Jack a few times the next few weeks, but we never got together. Late on the morning of July 16, 1996, the phone rang. It was Emily. Earlier that morning, Jack hadn't answered his phone, nor had he shown up at his usual breakfast hangout, so she went to his apartment on Vermont. There he was, apparently asleep in his bed, looking peaceful. After desperately trying to rouse him, she realized he was gone. She wanted to let me know before the press found out.

The pain of hearing this news overwhelmed me. I screamed, I cried, I cursed the heavens, I beat myself up for not attending his last play. I felt so lost.

Jack's funeral was held later that week. He was buried at Rose Hill Memorial Park in Whittier, a cemetery just outside of Los Angeles. I was given a personal invitation that entitled me to a special pass. Being in such an unstable state, a good friend offered to drive me. I'll never forget the miles of cars on the freeway with their headlights on, all paying tribute to Jack. It was so emotional. After the eulogy, and after the crowd dispersed, those close to Jack remained, and were each given a white rose to lay on his casket. When my turn came, I laid my rose down, tears flowing, and clung to that casket as if I could bring him back. Finally, two pallbearers gently removed me.

After the burial, Jack's Celebration of Life was held at the Los Angeles Theatre Center in downtown Los Angeles. Everyone who was anyone attended, but I stayed only a short time. I couldn't bear to hear his name. It was then I realized that he really was gone. Gone, but not forgotten.

Throughout the year, his music and plays were presented at festivals throughout the city. Then came his legacy. The Los Angeles Cultural Affairs dedicated the corner of Pico Boulevard and New Hampshire Avenue as C. Bernard Jackson Square, the birthplace of the ICCC. Officials nailed up the placket. It was so exciting and so appropriate. Emily and I and his close staff danced, cheered, and hugged each other. I think we all envisioned Jack smiling.

Afterwards, a tribute to the man, his music, and his mission was held at the Los Angeles Theatre Center, the same place his Celebration of Life was held over a year ago. This time, I participated in the festivities and enjoyed the accolades and stories about Jack, but tears still filled my eyes, and always do whenever there is talk about him.

I am one of the luckiest women on earth to have known and loved a man who once played the bongo drums at UCLA and rose to the stature of having his name engraved on a Los Angeles street. Some men are destined for greatness. Jack was one of them.

LADIES, DAMES, DIVAS, AND GALS

There is nothing like a dame, nothing in this world.

(Unlike my experiences with star actors, I never became friendly with any female megastars. I did enjoy the company of several well-established recognizable actresses and, more importantly, some wonderful friends who were working actresses. Almost all of them—note the word "almost"—contributed to my life and helped with my Hollywood career. In fact, the happiest times of my life were when my career was moving on up, and I was surrounded by these bright, fun, and beautiful ladies. We all, as they say, had each other's back.)

Helen Funai

A good friendship lasts for years. A great friendship lasts for fifty years. Lives change, there are ups and downs, but those friendships remain. This narrative is about the wonderful friendship I and Helen Funai, the lovely Japanese actress/dancer, had since meeting in 1972. We were introduced by my landlord, Howard Krieger, who was Helen's dance partner on *The Dean Martin Show* (1965–1974). Helen broke the barrier as the first Asian-American in the group of four actor/dancers called the Ding-A-Ling Sisters. She was drop-dead gorgeous, with hair to her waist, the face of a goddess, and a body in perpetual motion. Even before *The Dean Martin Show* she had accomplished an actor's dream with a major role, at age fifteen, in Broadway's *Flower Drum Song*

(1958–1960). Subsequently, she was crowned Miss Nisei (1963) and went on to do noteworthy films such as *Our Man Flint* (1966) and *A Funny thing Happened on the Way to the Forum* (1966). During this time, she also guested on popular television shows like *Bonanza* (1959–1973), *Bewitched* (1964–1972), *Mission: Impossible* (1966–1973), *Hawaii Five-O* (1968–1980), and others.

Soon after I met Helen, I landed a bit part on *The Carol Burnett Show* (1967–1978), which was shot in the CBS Television City complex next to the sound stage where *The Dean Martin Show* was taped. As chance would have it, and thanks to her dancing partner (and my landlord), Howard Krieger, we were introduced and went off to lunch together. She mentioned she represented a Japanese cosmetic company, and asked if I would be interested in working with her. The company wanted to expand into what was then referred to as the Caucasian market. I said yes. Soon, we were hosting cosmetic parties at fashionable homes. There was one problem: neither one of us was a saleswoman. We enlisted another friend of mine, a voluptuous actress named Nancy Fisher, who could sell snow to an Eskimo. It didn't work out, so we abandoned the project. By then, Helen and I were fast friends. We were a team.

In 1974, *The Dean Martin Show* was canceled. Helen was now free from daily rehearsals. I had already begun writing scripts, and Helen harbored a similar ambition. Believing in the adage strength in numbers, we decided to write together by day and have fun at night. We typed in the afternoons, pausing only to argue about dialogue or a character. We were very direct with each other, saying things like, "That's stupid," or "Your dialogue stinks." No offence was ever taken. It was a writing partner's dream relationship. Say it, argue it, type it, and print it. It worked! We sold a number of outlines to a producer friend of Helen's. One of our scripts focused on a priest's abuse of young boys. (Talk about being twenty years ahead of the times.)

Evenings and dinners were always fun. We would frequent fashionable restaurants or attempt to cook something at my house if we couldn't con some well-heeled guy into taking us both out. Helen had a slew of wealthy suitors. One in particular would pull up in his Rolls Royce and carry us off to some exclusive Beverly Hills restaurant. If we dined at a steak house, he would order special bones for my dogs. What a guy!

While madly writing, we did other things together, like shopping at the downtown garment district, and taking a six-week class in belly dancing. A fiasco, but a ton of fun. Helen, the consummate dancer, would watch me make a fool of myself, and say, "*Saaaaandy!*" I finally nailed it the last week. Her family included me in holiday celebrations, and I learned about Japanese cuisine. Her sister even guided me through real estate transactions.

On one occasion, we went to Las Vegas to see Juliet Prowse headline one of her shows. Helen was a good friend of the choreographer, who made sure we paid for nothing except gas. In hindsight, we should have paid for a plane ticket instead, as both of us are directionally handicapped. On our way to Vegas from Los Angeles, we stopped for coffee, then resumed our journey, not realizing that we were now heading *back* to Los Angeles. We drove for miles before this dawned on either of us. When we finally did make it to Las Vegas, we went to the wrong hotel.

Seeing Juliet Prowse onstage was a blast, but since Helen doesn't drink, smoke, or gamble, I was unable to show off my prowess in all three. That was Helen. (Even when she was doing *Flower Drum Song* in New York, she rarely partied with the cast.)

With my good friend,
actress/dancer Helen Funai.

Instead, we ate desserts and saw two more shows before heading home. Not exactly a "what happens in Vegas stays in Vegas" experience.

In 1977, Helen and I went to see *Saturday Night Fever*, which had just come out. We left the theater on a high. "I wanna go dancing," Helen said. "Where can we go? It's not safe downtown. Do you know anyone who has a membership to Pips?" (This was an elite membership-only disco club in Beverly Hills.)

Giving it some thought, I said, "Yeah, I know someone. Gene Erickson. I'll give him a call when we get back to my place. You'll like him. He's really nice, a self-made, blue-eyed, blond millionaire."

"*Saaaandy*, you make me sound like some Beverly Hills blond *bim*-bow."

"No, you're a beautiful Asian *bim*-bow." We laughed and bantered back and forth about our perfect dream man.

Later that evening, Gene called and graciously agreed to take us both to Pips, the Los Angeles nightclub of the moment. The following night, he and his friend Bob took us to dinner in Beverly Hills, then to Pips. Bob and I danced the night away. Helen and Gene seemed much more interested in each other than they did in dancing. Oh, they stepped out on the dance floor occasionally, but Helen, a professional dancer, kindly kept it very subdued, realizing that Gene didn't know his right foot from his left. Thus was born their forever romance, culminating a few years later in marriage.

In between their romance and subsequent marriage, Helen and I continued our acting careers and writing together. Somehow or other, we got the opportunity to submit a story outline about magic and murder to the producers of *Hawaii Five-O* (1968–1980). The next thing we knew, we had a writing contract with CBS. We were the first women writers ever to have such a contract. We worked with the story editor on our submission, but unfortunately, this legendary series was canceled in 1980 before our script was finished. On the positive side, the contract enabled me to join the Writers' Guild West, which was a real plus in my life.

Back to Helen. Gene's first marriage had been a failure, and he was hesitant to try again. But Helen, smart like a fox and a lady of steel, wasn't content to play the mistress. After several emotional breakups, Gene conceded, and they tied the knot in 1982. Soon after, they moved into the lovely Bel Air home Gene had built. I was happy for them, but it turned into a loss for me. In that less-enlightened era, Gene insisted that Helen give up her acting and writing careers and become a full-time Bel Air housewife. Although they never had children, she was a good stepmother to Gene's son, who was often a problem.

Helen and I remained close friends after her marriage, but it wasn't, and couldn't be, the same. She loved Gene, and enjoyed her new upscale life. In 2007, Gene sadly passed away from cancer. Helen fell apart for about a year, then came back like thunder. Our friendship was refreshed and reinvigorated, and we again began seeing quite a lot of each other. Unfortunately, we never resumed our writing partnership. It just wasn't in the cards. Helen was busy with her social life, and my acting career had heated up.

Now in our so-called golden years, we both are so grateful for our longtime friendship. We are still there for each other, and always will be, even if we don't always see eye to eye. Helen never introduces me to someone without proudly saying, "She introduced me to Gene."

Jacquie, Meg, and Me

In the mid-1980s, I joined The Actor's Lab, a scene study class in Los Angeles run by Tony Award nominee Frederick Combs, who starred in *A Taste of Honey* and *The Boys in the Band* on Broadway. He was also a prodigy of the renowned acting coach Uta Hagen. It was the best workshop I ever attended. Among the diverse and talented actors in the class were Jacqueline Schultz (Jacquie) and Megan Wittner (Meg). The three of us hit it off immediately. There was no actors' competition among us, perhaps because we were all approximately five years apart in age, or just because of who we were and the values that were instilled in us.

I was the oldest, with dark-brown hair. Then came Meg, with auburn hair, and Jacquie, a natural blond. Meg was not only a stunner, but had a social touch that could open any door. Jacquie was an unbelievable talent, and beautiful inside and out. Yeah, I too was talented and beautiful, if not quite as successful. The three of us started doing scenes together, borrowing each other's clothes, referring each other to photographers, hairdressers, doctors, and/or just simply hanging out. Whoever had the last job paid for Happy Hour or dinner. That was an unwritten code. Birthdays and holidays were always celebrated at one of our homes, because none of us had any family in Los Angeles. *We* were family.

Meg was the queen of commercials in both New York and Los Angeles. She appeared in hundreds of ads, playing the quintessential young housewife or mother. Every time you turned on the television, there she was promoting something. One day at Meg's house, I whined about my commercial agent. Without a moment's hesitation, she called her agent and raved about my commercial capabilities, which immediately led to an appointment. We poured wine, tossed our clothes to the wind, and jumped into her hot tub. Soon after, Meg threw me a surprise birthday party and invited anyone who was someone so that career connections could be made. She was always available to help in whatever way she could. Her biggest setback was her health and emotional neediness, which slowed her career. But she had an untrained talent, not to mention photogenic looks. At moments, she could be almost brilliant.

Jacquie, on the other hand, was an amazing actress with a wonderful laugh. Working with her in our scene study class was always an inspiration. She would nail the character and have the lines down by our second rehearsal. When she auditioned for a guest-starring part on a television show, three out of four times she'd book it. Yet she was very modest about her success. She never

With my partner in crime, Jacqueline Schultz.

told me that back in New York, prior to moving to Hollywood, she was a star on the soap *As the World Turns* (1956–2010). I found that out when we both were asked to judge an amateur acting competition at the Los Angles Inner City Culture Center. Upon arriving at the event, she was recognized and mobbed. I was stunned. She had mentioned once that she had worked on a New York soap, but not that she was one of the stars. During this time, Jacquie and I became incredibly close personally and professionally. As the months passed, we took several additional acting workshops together, two classes at The Improv and Salome Jens' scene study class. Jacquie, like Meg, introduced me to her theatrical agent, who subsequently signed me, although it didn't work out.

Our friendship was a two-way street: give and take. Jacquie once took a bad fall doing a chase scene while guest-starring on the police show *Hunter* (1984–1991). She called me when she got home, clearly in great pain. I rushed to her apartment, where I found her unable to move, her foot propped on a chair. Her ankle was the color of a rainbow and the size of an elephant's leg. Over her objections, I immediately took her to the emergency room. X-rays revealed a badly broken ankle, necessitating a huge cast being put on it. Jacquie was told to stay off it and keep it elevated. I took her to the doctor and brought her groceries and videos almost every day for the next two weeks. She was so appreciative and never complained. The *Hunter* production company covered all her medical expenses, but as far as I know never compensated her for the month of work lost on other shows she otherwise would have done. Jacquie being Jacquie, a few months later, she was back in front of the camera and in real life running the Los Angeles marathon. She made it to the finish line!

Good things often end, and so did our mighty threesome. Life changes, and folks move on. It's the nature of things. Meg found her true love, they had a baby, and she slowly retired from acting. Jacquie also found true love. She married Steven Sachs, the Artistic Director of the Fountain Theatre in Los Angeles, and they had two sons. I was maid of honor at her wedding, and threw her an Italian wedding reception. She continued her successful acting career for more than ten years, winning several Ovation Awards. (The equivalent to the New York Off-Broadway Theater Awards.) Later in life, she gave up acting and got her master's degree in child psychology, specializing in autism.

Things changed as the years went on. My friendship with Meg slowly faded, but my love and friendship with Jacquie merely took a hiatus while she devoted herself to her family. The children are grown, and now we are back on the mark, enjoying each other's company almost weekly. (There is a God.)

I treasure the time and support all three of us gave each other when we were actively part of the Hollywood scene. To quote the song crooned by Bing Crosby and Frank Sinatra in *High Society* (1956), "What an elegant, swellegant party it was."

Joyce Bulifant

Teenage best friends are so intense. It's that coming-of-age time in one's life when everything is so important and *must* be shared. Sometimes these friendships remain steadfast for a lifetime; other times, they fade away forever; sometimes they take a break and later come full circle. The latter describes my friendship with the fun-loving actress Joyce Bulifant.

Joyce and I met at Solebury in 1953. It was a small coed boarding school in New Hope, Pennsylvania. She was fifteen and I was fourteen, both of us in our sophomore year. She had already been there for a couple of years when I arrived with Holly, my white Labrador Retriever. (In today's vernacular, a therapy dog.) It didn't take long for me to realize that, in spite of Joyce's youth, she was the "it" girl on campus. She was blond and petite, full of fun, with a high, girlish voice, and the youngest member of the cheerleading squad. Everyone loved her.

Being a good dancer and an excellent tumbler, I was soon accepted in the cheerleading squad, which was comprised mostly of juniors and seniors, making Joyce and me the youngest members. We had the same creative interests, and a strong friendship ensued. We took classes together, went to a weekly dance class off-campus, and spent many a night devising teenage pranks and dreaming of becoming actresses.

The first year I was at Solebury, I had the room next to Joyce's, but for the last two years we roomed together and shared it with my dog. Holly was the perfect canine—smart, obedient, and

High school pals—together again.

affectionate—but being an inside-outside dog, she shed. This made Joyce a crazy person. On the other hand, I would become infuriated whenever Joyce stuffed everything in our joint closet before clean-up inspection on Saturdays, which caused us both to be grounded. Saturdays were special, because they were free days, and all of us students would dash off to the nearby picturesque town of New Hope. We would first go to the local movie, and then to the nearby coffee shop, and spend our allowance on burgers, sodas, and the jukebox.

About this time, Joyce started seriously dating a classmate of ours, James (Jimmy) MacArthur, son of Helen Hayes, the First Lady of the American Theater and Charles MacArthur, the noted Broadway playwright and screenwriter (whose credits included 1939's *Wuthering Heights*). They visited Solebury often and would invite all of us out to dinner. I always tried to sit by Mr. MacArthur. He was quick and funny and so much fun. Miss Hayes took a real liking to Joyce, cementing her and Jimmy's romance. Life began to change, especially for Joyce.

During this time, Miss Hayes did a benefit performance titled *An Evening of Queens* at Solebury. Joyce and I were cast as ladies-in-waiting for one of the four queens Miss Hayes played. Yep, I worked with the First Lady of the American Theater.

After we graduated and received our diplomas (yes, including my dog, Holly), Joyce went on to study at the American Academy of Performing Arts, and I went to Bard College in upstate New York, where I majored in acting. I often returned to New York City to work as a background dancer on *The Arthur Murray Party* (1950–1960), a television variety show. My mother, the lead dancer on the show, arranged for Joyce to also dance on it. We were together again!

Less than two years later, I dropped out of college and moved to Los Angeles. There, I married a med student, temporarily giving up my ambitions to be an actor, and became a nine-to-five clerical worker. Joyce finished her studies, moved into my vacated New York West Side studio apartment, above my parents, and embarked upon whirlwind adventures on the national and international celebrity circuit. Soon thereafter, she married Jimmy. Neither my parents nor I was invited to the ceremony, which stung when I read about it. Say what? Yep, Joyce's life had taken a storybook turn. Jimmy later achieved fame for his role as Dan ("Book 'em, Danno") Williams, second in command to Jack Lord's Steve McGarrett on the long-running hit police show *Hawaii Five-O* (1968–1980).

Before you could say "stand by, rolling, action," she was in Hollywood and landing parts in numerous television shows, including *Perry Mason* (1957–1966), *Naked City* (1958–1963), *Bonanza* (1959–1973), and, later, in the long-running *The Mary Tyler Moore Show* (1970–1977) as Marie, Gavin MacLeod's wife. Joyce was living her dream: happy, successful, creatively fulfilled.

Reality intervened in 1968. We both got divorced, she from Jimmy, and I from my doctor. With considerable relief, I resumed my acting career. I began studying with the demanding Stanford Meisner at the Neighborhood Playhouse in New York, then returned to Hollywood. Within a few short years, I was a working actress traveling in similar social circles as Joyce. She continued acting, and married several important Hollywood men. Unfortunately, our paths never crossed during this time, in spite of the fact that at one point we lived just a few blocks apart in Hancock Park, did many of the same TV shows, and knew and socialized with many of the same folks. We met once for lunch, but that was it. The actor Roger Perry, her last husband and love of her life from earlier years, and I had the same agent. Earlier, when he was married to the comedian Jo Anne Worley, our mutual agent would often take me to cocktail parties at their house, where the vodka flowed.

Joyce's career slowed down through the 1980s and 1990s. Now married to William Asher, the producer of *Bewitched* (1964–1972), she devoted her time to being a mother to his and her children. They lived in Benedict Canyon close to Beverly Glen's elite shopping center, a place I often patronized, and where she visited daily to pick up her mail. We ran into each other there once, but exchanged only a few words before she split.

Fast forward to 2006 and the 50th anniversary of our graduating class from Solebury. There we were, at Solebury again. Right back where we started from! Joyce and Roger were now married, and we all spent almost every moment together that weekend. We laughed, we reminisced, and filled in the years we had lost. Our friendship was renewed, and we bonded.

Joyce later wrote a book, aptly named *My Four Hollywood Husbands*, which I read with delight, because it was Joyce in a book. I could hear her girlish voice, smile at her innocent mistakes, and admire her tenacity.

At this stage in our lives, Joyce and I email back and forth, and occasionally get together either in Palm Springs, where she now lives, or in Studio City, where I live. Our hiatus is over. We have come full circle.

Cher

Cher, an entertainment superstar.

In a professional weekly dance class headed by the choreographer Bob Banas, in or around 1970, a somewhat awkward, tall, dark-haired girl stood beside me moving left and right to the count of 5, 6, 7, 8. She always arrived with a small following of female dancers/friends. None of us could match the proficiency of the other dancers. I soon learned that the dark-haired girl was Cher, already an established singer and soon to become co-star of the successful television show, *The Sonny and Cher Comedy Hour* (1971–1974) with her husband, the equally famous Sonny Bono. We never really spoke, just nodded at each other in passing.

Flash forward to 1976. *The Sonny and Cher Comedy Hour,* having been canceled in 1974, was reincarnated as *The Sonny and Cher Show* (1976–1977) in more of a variety-program format. I had lucked out and was renting a very small house in West Hollywood owned by Ret Turner, Bob Mackie's partner and head of wardrobe at CBS Television City, where all of CBS's variety and musical shows were shot. (See chapter on Ret Turner). As is well-known, Bob designed all of Cher's outstanding costumes, but Ret made them happen.

One day, Ret phoned me from CBS in a bit of a panic, and asked if I would come down to the studio for a couple of hours and help watch Chastity, Sonny and Cher's daughter. Ret and his crew were frantically trying to finish some costumes before the show taped, and didn't have time to babysit, something they quite often did because Chastity preferred hanging out with CBS folks rather than a nanny.

When I arrived, I was introduced to Chastity (now Chaz), then a picture postcard of a five-year-old girl: blond curly hair and an open smile. We clicked. Soon, she was showing me all the cute and beautiful dresses "Uncle Ret" had made for her. We decided to go to Farmer's Market for lunch. Ret cleared it with Cher, and off we went, accompanied by two male dancers. We had a fun lunch, with Chastity running around ordering ice cream and deserts. Afterwards, I returned her to Ret. Cher, standing nearby while being fitted, mechanically thanked me. This scenario played out several more times until the show was canceled, ending my babysitting gig. I had hoped to remind Cher that we had taken Bob Banas' dance class together a few years earlier, but the opportunity never arose.

Cher, of course, went on to become a superstar, winning an Oscar for *Moonstruck* (1987) and a Grammy for the album *Believe* (1998), not to mention her highly acclaimed television specials and Las Vegas shows. Through all of this she remained devoted to Ret, who every year staged an elegant open house Christmas Day party. Everyone was invited, from the stars to the gardener. One year, Cher arrived and presented Ret with a diamond earring. Since I was standing beside him, he graciously reintroduced me. Cher just glanced at me and said, in a flat voice, "Hello." Granted, it was a party, and time had long passed since I had so happily and responsibly babysat Chastity, but I did expect at least a complete sentence. No such luck. As quickly as Cher entered, she was gone.

Ret died in 2016, after suffering terribly from cancer for almost a year. His funeral was a small, intimate affair at Forest Lawn. Only about 25 people were present. Cher, dressed in black and looking lovely, was one of the attendees. She seemed genuinely sad, and talked to no one. Actually, no one talked to anyone. We all were in mourning for this wonderful man.

Several weeks later, a Celebration of Life was held for Ret at his favorite Jewish Temple downtown. This event was packed with hundreds of folks. There again, weaving through the crowd, was Cher. I didn't deign to approach her, nor did anyone else that I recall. Seeing her this time, however, I stood in awe of this charismatic, beautiful, and talented individual who found the time, and felt the need, to honor her old friend Ret. I think he would have been so pleased. Obviously, she is so much more than the icon the public sees.

Brenda Venus

Sometime in the early 1970s, I moved out of the house I was renting from Ret Turner, and into a cute "mini palace" next door (in actuality a bungalow), also owned by Ret. While his assistant, Leslie Levitt, and I got my old house ready to rent, Brenda Venus, a sexy, beautiful actress, and a fellow member of the Melrose Acting Workshop, was frantically looking for a place to live. Her apartment building had just been condemned due to a major fire. Brenda drove a black, shiny Jaguar, and from all appearances seemed quite reliable, thanks in part to her abundance of southern charm. She appeared to be a good prospective renter. I gave her information to Ret, who said, "Fine! The rent is $450. First and last month, and she can move in whenever she wants. Just take care of it. I'm too busy to be bothered." That was so Ret.

A moving van arrived within the next few days. Brenda busied herself decorating and calling me constantly about one thing or another. A few weeks later, her mother, Mrs. Venus, a well-honed southern lady, came to visit. Before leaving to return home, she gave me her phone number in case of an emergency.

Not long after Brenda moved in, I noticed that men in shiny black limos were visiting her with almost clockwork regularity. I didn't give this much thought at first. After all, what successful man in their right mind wouldn't want to date her? She was stunningly gorgeous, and was possessed of a sexy, southern charm that just wouldn't quit.

Brenda called one day and asked if I wouldn't mind going to dinner that evening with the driver of a celebrity friend she had invited to dinner. She wanted to spend some special time with this friend without being concerned about the driver waiting

The enigmatic Brenda Venus.

around. She would make reservations for us at Dan Tana's, then as now a famous celebrity hangout on Santa Monica Boulevard. Of course, I said yes.

That night, dressed to the nines (at least in my mind), I walked over to Brenda's. I had just arrived when a black limousine arrived, and out stepped a megastar cultural icon well on his way to receiving multiple Academy Awards in both acting and directing. (I won't mention his name, because he's still alive and I don't care to be sued. Let's just call him a man with no name.) The driver and I exchanged polite chit-chat, then drove to Dan Tana's and spent a leisurely two hours. He was a nice guy, and we had a good time, but discussion of his boss was strictly off-limits. One has to admire and respect that kind of loyalty. As I crawled into bed that night, I wondered if I had read the evening's scenario correctly. Were Brenda and her famous visitor really just having dinner, or was something else going on? Something classically Hollywood. Then it occurred to me that it was none of my business. It was Brenda's life. Besides, I could be wrong.

A few weeks later, Brenda called out of the blue, asking if I would lower her rent. I quickly and firmly replied, "No. Your rent is more than reasonable. Actually, unheard of in this area."

"Okay, just thought I would ask," she said, and hung up.

I learned later that she then went directly to Ret with a sob story about her finances, not mentioning that she had approached me and been turned down. Ret being Ret lowered her rent fifty dollars. I was livid.

Late one evening three weeks later, I heard men's voices and the sound of a truck coming from Brenda's house, which was next door to mine. This seemed odd, but I ignored it. The next morning while walking my dogs, I noticed her front door was wide open. I poked my head in . . . and my jaw dropped. The place was empty. The furniture was gone, everything was gone, even the shower curtain rod was gone. What was left was a mess. The walls were disfigured with large and small holes, and the rug was strewn with dirt and paper. Worst of all, the new built-in air conditioner Ret had recently purchased was also gone, leaving a huge hole in the living room wall.

I called Ret in a fury. He said he'd be home after work, and we could talk about it then. I tried to track Brenda down. She didn't answer her phone. I didn't know any of her friends, so I could not contact them. I did reach her agent, who told me she couldn't legally give out a client's personal phone number, but said she would call Brenda and tell her I wanted to talk with her. A dead end all around.

Then I remembered Brenda's mother, Mrs. Venus of Mississippi, who had given me her number when last she visited. I dialed her up and described the carnage. She seemed genuinely concerned and confused, and promised to check with Brenda and get back to me.

True to her word, she called back shortly thereafter in a clearly emotional state, her accent accentuating the southern belle in her. She stated that Brenda had suddenly moved out in order to promptly move in with some famous writer whose last name was Miller. She couldn't remember the first name.

"Arthur Miller?" I asked.

"That might be him, but it doesn't sound quite right," she replied.

"Well, no, it can't be, as Arthur Miller is married and lives in New York," I muttered. Then, my brain in overdrive, it suddenly hit me. Brenda had moved in with *Henry* Miller, the only other living famous writer with a last name of Miller. He was the celebrated author of *Tropic of Cancer* (1934), the infamous book that was banned in almost every country for its explicit sexual content. A far cry indeed from the award-winning playwright Arthur Miller. Obviously, Mrs. Venus wasn't familiar with the works of either Miller. I could have set her straight, but she seemed upset enough already without me adding fuel to the fire. A lengthy conversation, seasoned with tears and apologies, led to Brenda's mom agreeing to pay for the damages to the house, which she subsequently and graciously did. Over dinner that evening with Ret, I recounted the day's saga. He was pleased and amused that I had handled the ugly situation so well.

Several days later, in the dead of night (naturally), Brenda's henchmen returned the air conditioner, unceremoniously dumping it on the front porch. I never saw or spoke to Brenda Venus again. Henry Miller in 1986 published the book, *Dear, Dear Brenda: The Love Letters of Henry Miller to Brenda Venus,* but she was anything but dear to me. Taking advantage of Ret's generosity was totally unacceptable in my book. Narcissistic folks and users are often hard to identify due to their charm and/or charisma, and I sure missed this one.

Joanna Kerns

Here's a dynamite lady who has it all. She's not only a lovely working actress, but a woman who has transitioned into the director's chair, helping to break the longstanding tradition that only men could and should direct. Joanna's acting career began in the 1970s with guest-starring roles on such shows as *The Love Boat* (1976–1986) and *Charlie's Angels* (1976–1981) before gaining a larger profile co-starring on the domestic sitcom *Growing Pains* (1985–1992), which brought America the Seaver family. After that show ended, Joanna concentrated more on directing, although she still appears in front of the camera.

Joanna Kerns, a great lady,
actress and director.

I met Joanna in 1989 when I was cast as Betty, a young grandma, on an episode of *Growing Pains*. This represented a much-appreciated five-day's work. I was thrilled to play the mother of a teenage girl who was dating Mike (Kirk Cameron), the oldest child in the Seaver clan. The narrative catch was that my teenage daughter had a two-year-old love child. This caused, shall we say, some angst in this fictional family.

Growing Pains was shot on tape, which means the director typically doesn't personally interact with the actors, but directs them while watching the action unfold on a monitor. The only time I remember meeting this director was on the first day's read-through with the full cast. The next few days were filled with indoor and outdoor shots, some of which I was in, some I was not. Although everyone was pleasant and professional, there seemed to be some tension in the air. Perhaps this was caused by the director, or by Kirk Cameron's coming-of-age teenage independence. I never found out.

Not helping my nerves was the director's habit of constantly referring to me as Grandma. I was in my forties and age-sensitive, so this did not endear me to him. He would shout from the booth above the stage, with directions such as, "Grandma, pick up the toy as you enter!" The third time this happened, I played dumb and pretended not to know to whom he was speaking. When he repeated the patronizing address, I said, "Oh, you mean me. Sandra! I'm sorry." He didn't get it, but Joanna did. Out of the corner of my eye, I saw her smile, look down, and stifle a laugh.

After the shot was in the can, Joanna walked over to me and said, "I love your hair. It's just beautiful."

"Thank you. I wish the director did," I responded with a halfhearted smile.

"Hey, it's okay. He should know your name; you've been here almost a week. Let's have a cup of coffee, and you can tell me where you get your hair done."

We quickly established camaraderie over that cup of coffee, chatting like girlfriends do about our likes and dislikes, fashion, and, of course, hair. I gave her my stylist's name and address, and Joanna in fact went to him. During our conversation I mentioned that I was troubled because the only other guest actor on set, who had just a three-line part, was blatantly pilfering everything from food to hi-liters to paper clips, and if it was noticed I was afraid I might be accused.

Joanna favored me again with that warm smile, and said, "We all saw her, but I doubt if it will be an issue. It happens now and again, but it's in the budget." That stunned me. Working actors stealing things on set had never occurred to me.

The next day was the final day of the shoot. Wouldn't you know it? That director did it again. "Grandma, face the teddy bear you're holding out to the camera!" he yelled. This was my last scene, and I knew I couldn't be replaced or they would have had to reshoot the entire show. So, I fired back.

"My name is *Sandra*, and I play the *grandma*, but that is *not* my name. I've been here five days, and you have yet to call me by my name, which is *Sandra!*" Silence. Thirty seconds later, a somewhat contrite voice emanated from the director's booth: "Sandra, would you. . . ." On the last day, he finally got it.

I never met Joanna again, but I have avidly followed her career. It's always a bit difficult guesting on a show, because everything and everyone is new. The regulars have it down to a science. Stars like Joanna make it easier. They are and should always be lauded for their talent and kindness to other working guest actors. They are a gift.

Jennifer Rhodes

Jennifer and me looking for dates on New Year's.

Jennifer is the quintessential stereotype of the successful working actress. She's attractive, talented, and tenacious. No one or anything gets in her way. She is also a diva, but in a fun, outrageous way. She loves being the center of attention, and with her quick wit, she usually is. She's racked up about 90 film and television credits spanning 40 years. Broad comedy and satire are her forte, as seen by her performances in the television series *Grace and Frankie* (2015–2022) and her recurring role as "Grams" in *Charmed* (1998–2006), not to mention her hysterical role in the horror film *Night of the Demons 2* (1994). Earlier in her career, she played it down a peg, as Winona Ryder's mother in the highly acclaimed film *Heathers* (1988).

I first met Jennifer when I joined the Melrose Theatre in the early 1970s. She was then the queen of the Melrose, well on her way to becoming a diva. I didn't like her, and stayed clear of her. Several months after joining the theatre, a production titled *The Kitty Genovese Story* moved from the Music Center's Mark Taper Forum in downtown Los Angeles to the Melrose. It was an ensemble play written by author/journalist William B. Murray (Bill), soon to become the love of my life. Jennifer was cast in the lead role. She was wonderful, and both she and the play got rave reviews. As rehearsals got underway, I found myself amused by her antics and admired her ability to justify any and all problems related to her. At moments, she was irresistible, and it wasn't long before we became friends. Not good friends, just friends.

By the time the play opened, Bill and I were a fixture. At the same time, both Jennifer's and my career started to take off. Several months after the play closed, Bill got a two-year contract as the American editor of the Italian version of *Playboy*. Off we went to Rome. I returned to Los Angeles every couple of months for an acting job and to take care of domestic affairs. Of course, I checked in at the Melrose, and even did a short-run, three-act play about the stages of love: I played Eve in Mark Twain's *The Apple Tree*. Jennifer did a more sophisticated modern play. Another success for us both.

A year or so later, *la dolce vita* came to an end. Sadly, so did my relationship with Bill. I was devastated, still am. I returned to the Melrose, only to find it even more elitist than when I had last been there. Soon, things turned ugly over some vignettes I had partially written and was scheduled to act in. Jennifer and Paul Kent, the theater's artistic director, ruled supreme, and I was removed from the project. That did it. I walked away from the Melrose and never returned. It also ended my quasi-friendship with Jennifer.

Ten years passed. I was asked to audition to understudy the lead in a play at the Mark Taper Forum, and there was Jennifer trying out for the same role. Neither of us booked it. But after we both auditioned, Jennifer approached and asked if she could buy me a drink at the Itchy Foot Café down the street. I hesitated, but agreed. One of the best decisions I've ever made. We ordered wine, well, several wines. We talked about our lives and our careers, and, of course, the Melrose Theatre incident. She cried, I cried, we promised to never again interfere negatively with each other's career, and in the future to support each other in any way possible. Thus, a lifelong friendship with Jennifer finally came to fruition.

Jennifer and I both continued our careers, and our friendship grew. We've had our moments, but we're always there for each other when the chips are down. Yeah, she's still a diva, but now there's not only mutual respect, but love. What could be better?

I've Seen Her. What's Her Name?

Through my forty-plus years in the Biz, I've met countless talented actresses and wannabe actresses. They all started out with a dream, but all too often lacked training, tenacity, and/or any sense of reality. Some actually believed they would be discovered on Sunset Boulevard. Or that they could get a lead role in a major film if they met or sent their picture to the right producer or director. Or, worst of all, believed the way to stardom was a roll in the hay with almost anyone with an industry title. Still others would unconsciously sabotage opportunities by being chronically late, or dressed inappropriately, or being too desperate.

But this brief heading is not about those actors that failed for whatever reason. It's about the winners who just never really caught the right break. They are the backbone of Hollywood. Emily Yancy (see C. Bernard Jackson chapter), Jeanine Anderson, Katherine Disque, Marcia Moran, Carol Wyand (voiceover talent). They all fall into this special category. All these ladies can and have been seen on television and in films. They all have strong resumes, substantial screen credits, and solid stage credits. Yes, you've seen them, and these are just a few of their names. Thumbs up to all working actors, especially if they are women.

QUINN MARTIN (The Producer)

1922–1987

Some weeks in Hollywood, you hit the trifecta. This was my week. I had appeared on a hit television show, my true love had returned from Rome, and I had a winner at the racetrack.

(The producer Quinn Martin was the Dick Wolf of his era. His company, QM Productions, dominated action/adventure network television from the late 1960s through the early 1980s. He developed and perfected his own unique formula for such successful one-hour television series as The Untouchables *(1959–1963),* The Fugitive *(1963–1967),* The F.B.I. *(1965–1974),* The Invaders *(1967–1968),* Cannon *(1971–1976),* The Streets of San Francisco *(1972–1977),* Barnaby Jones *(1973–1980), and many more. In 1997, he was honored with membership into the Television Hall of Fame. When not working, Mr. Martin could be found at the racetrack, urging his stable of thoroughbreds on to the finish line.)*

I've Got the Horse Right Here!

My main squeeze, the writer William B. Murray (Bill to everyone), had just flown home from an extended magazine assignment in Rome. It was 1972. I was jazzed to have him back and anxious to hear about Rome and read his story. No matter what genre or format he wrote in, the results were exceptional. Making my week even better, I had just finished shooting an episode of

The F.B.I., a show produced by Quinn Martin. It was only a featured part, but I hoped it would lead to many more opportunities.

Back to Bill. He was a talented and exciting man. He didn't just write, he sang and loved opera, wrote and directed plays, adored his children, and possessed a sardonic wit. His greatest passion was the racetrack. (Don't tell his kids.) Yep, he really loved the track! The day after he returned, we were off to Santa Anita Park in Los Angeles for a day at the races. Of course, we stopped at the local newsstand for the daily racing form, which Bill frantically marked up with his lucky pencil while somehow simultaneously driving his sports car.

The drive alone was exciting. Leaving his car in the exclusive press parking area (ah, perks), we joined his track buddies in the clubhouse. Bill tipped the usher for a box seat, handed me an official racing program, and got down to the serious business of picking winners. I hung out awhile with him, then went to the paddock to visit the horses and watch them get saddled up for the first race. That's always a thrill, with horses, jockeys, trainers, and owners all intently convened, giving and getting last-minute advice. I moseyed back to the clubhouse and began picking winners for my $2.00 and $5.00 bets. I always picked horses according to their crazy names, their physical attributes—like the length of their tails—and their jockeys' colors, all of which drove Bill nuts.

He and his cohorts tirelessly tried to school me in their racing acumen, to no avail. I admit that I rarely won, but I always had fun. It was just a day at the track, replete with great company, good food, and, of course, plenty of vino.

Peeling through my program, I noticed a horse in the eighth race named Orange Juice, owned by none other than Quinn

Television producer Quinn Martin.

Martin. (Insert proverbial light bulb image here.) It was a long shot. A *really* long shot: 23-1. I showed Bill, and told him I was going to put $5 to win on Orange Juice. He shook his head and rolled his eyes. "Don't be a fool. That horse hasn't got a chance."

"But it's Quinn Martin's horse. He just gave me a job last week. The *least* I can do is bet on his horse," I countered.

"Well, if you must, then at least bet him to show, not to win."

"Nope, I'm betting him to win."

"Okay, throw your money away," he said disgustedly, and rejoined his cronies.

The day was almost over when the eighth race was called. I waited to place my bet until the horses were on the track. Orange Juice, a sorrel, looked so beautiful and proud to be out there with the more elite horses. I blew him a kiss, marched to the betting window, and plunked my five bucks down on Orange Juice to win. The clerk behind the window didn't even look up, just muttered an ironic "Good luck," and handed me my ticket.

Back in my box seat, I sat tensely until the loudspeaker announced, "The horses are in the gate . . . and they're off!"

I jumped to my feet at the same instant the horses broke out of the gate, screaming and yelling like a madwoman. "Go get 'em, Orange Juice! C'mon, Orange Juice! Get it in gear! Go, go, go!" I whooped and hollered and cajoled and caterwauled. It seemed the more I screamed, the faster he went. Halfway around the track, OJ was in third place, then second place.

"You're almost home, Orange Juice! You can do it! I know you can!" I screamed.

Suddenly, Orange Juice was at the finish line, crossing the wire in front of all the other horses, in first place, numero uno, the long-shot winner!

A shocked, disbelieving buzz resounded around the track. The seasoned pros, my Bill included, shook their heads, moaned in anguish, and wondered what in the equine blazes had just happened.

I, on the other hand, screamed with joy. "I've got the *winner!*"

Waving my ticket in Bill's face (a little ungracious, I admit), I rushed off to collect my winnings. Call it intuition or inspiration or chutzpah, my loyalty pick netted me over $100, something of a fortune for me. Thankfully, I didn't bet on the last race, but instead went down to the paddock and personally thanked Orange Juice. I swear he winked at me.

I took Bill to dinner that night on my winnings, then sat down and wrote Quinn Martin a short note. I thanked him for my recent gig on *The F.B.I.* and told him I had bet on his horse Orange Juice to win, and now the rent was paid.

A week or so later, I auditioned for a part on *Barnaby Jones*, another QM Production. The reading went well, but nothing to write home about. Somewhat to my surprise, and of course delight, my agent phoned the next day to say I had booked the job. An hour later, Dodi McLean, the casting director and a new friend of mine, also called. She laughed, and said, "So, you bet on Quinn Martin's horses." I didn't catch on, then Dodi explained.

She and another CD were at their weekly meeting with Quinn to discuss casting for his many shows. Quinn was a hands-on producer and involved in all aspects of his programs. Dodi and the other casting director laid out on his desk pictures and resumes of attractive gals they had narrowed down for a part on *Barnaby Jones*. He shuffled through them quickly, then pushed my picture forward and said, "Her."

The other casting director obviously had another actress in mind, and somewhat disappointedly asked, "Why her?"

Without a moment's hesitation, Quinn Martin answered, "She bets on my horses."

Fate played a hand in all this, because I not only landed that role, but did five other *Barnaby Jones* episodes over the next few years, plus a *Cannon*, all of them prestigious QM Productions. (Unfortunately, I never booked a *Streets of San Francisco*. Probably because San Francisco doesn't have a racetrack.)

Also, word apparently came down from upstairs that I was someone special, and was always to be treated like someone special. Even my paycheck improved with each show. One morning in the middle of a QM shoot my car wouldn't start. Luckily,

Wingo, my gardener, drove me to the studio in his old green pickup. I apologized to the director for being late, and explained why. The next thing I knew my car was picked up from my home by some crew member, taken to a garage, repaired, and returned to the lot—all charges paid in full. Stars get this treatment, but I wasn't a star or even a regular, just an actor doing a few days' work on a show.

Regrettably, I never personally met Quinn Martin. I would like to have thanked him for helping me pay my rent for years and, of course, to talk horses. There you go. One never knows how and why one gets a job in Tinseltown.

Obviously, one just has to bet on the right horse, of course.

RICARDO MONTALBAN

1920–2009

Some people have only to enter a room, and everyone instantly knows they have arrived. One such actor was Ricardo Montalban, whose charm, charisma, and carriage made him stand out in any setting. He was also one of Hollywood's kindest gentlemen, who came to my rescue in a rather public fashion in 1985.

(Born in Mexico City in 1920, Ricardo Montalban came to the United States as a teenager and began his theatrical career in New York as an actor and dancer. He soon migrated to Hollywood and became a working actor, featured mainly in Hispanic and other ethnic parts. By the late 1940s–early 1950s, he was a leading man, starring alongside such notable actresses as Esther Williams, June Allyson, and Jane Powell. Being the epitome of the "Latin Lover," however, hampered his film career. He even did a film titled Latin Lovers *(1953)! Montalban did periodically appear in interesting films, while often returning to the New York stage. Broadway was good to him. He even earned a 1958 Tony nomination as best actor in a musical for* Jamaica. *Proud of his Spanish heritage, in 1970 he created Nosotros, the Los Angeles-based theater company that provided opportunities for Latinos working in the film industry. The company still thrives today. His public profile was at its highest during the run of the hit television series* Fantasy Island*

(1977–1984). He followed that with solid work on The Colbys *(1985–1987), as well as numerous guest-starring roles in other top shows.)*

My Dancing "Save" by Ricardo

Every decade has its notable fitness fad—roller derby in the 1950s, calisthenics in the 1960s, treadmills in the 1970s. In the 1980s, dance aerobics was *the* fitness craze. (Thank you, Jane Fonda.) In the middle of that decade, I was swept up in this fitness zeitgeist, along with several of my acting friends, as we found ourselves attending dance aerobics classes three times weekly at the Hollywood YMCA. Our particular class was led by a well-known older dancer and filled with a diversity of show-biz folks.

Several months into our weekly routine, a middle-aged woman named Aida approached me. Without preamble, she said, "Obviously, you used to be a dancer."

Slightly taken aback by her powers of observation, I replied, "Yes, but that was years ago. I don't dance professionally anymore. Now I make a living just acting."

"Well, you move like a dancer, and with those long legs, you're striking."

"Thank you," I answered modestly.

Aida paused, as if sizing me up, before continuing. "I'm a choreographer, and I've been hired to do the choreography for the Edwin Lester Tribute at the Dorothy Chandler Pavilion at the Music Center. It's to be a one-night celebration."

I was impressed. Edwin Lester was the founder and longtime director of the Civil Light Opera at the Music Center. Under his forty-year tutorship it was widely considered the best-run production company in the world. This was to be a tribute to him on his 90th birthday.

"I'd like you to be part of the dance chorus," Aida went on. "It pays $100, and all expenses. You'll have a chance to meet many of the world's greatest musical entertainers. It's a big gala complete with a great wrap party. Are you interested?"

"Yes, of course," I answered excitedly, "but I haven't danced professionally in years, and I might not be up to it."

"Oh, you'll be fine. They want older dancers, so that the celebrities don't look too old. It's not going to be a Michael Jackson video. It's a three-day gig. The first day we'll set the dance routine, the second day will be a full rehearsal with the musical director, celebrities, and the orchestra. On the third day there will be a run-through, dress rehearsal, and then showtime. Does that work for you?"

Buoyed by her evident belief in my ability, I nodded enthusiastically. Aida gave me the dates, we exchanged contact information, and off she went.

I regaled my acting pals with the good news over coffee, went home, and immediately began stretching exercises. I was sweating like a marathon runner when my then husband arrived. He gawped at me for a moment, then asked, "Are you training to run away from home?" (I loved his sense of humor.)

"I got a job dancing at the Music Center, through my class at the YMCA, no less," I replied. "Can you believe it? I'm going to dance at the Music Center."

He laughed, congratulated me, and poured himself a drink. I babbled on, mentioning it was for the Edwin Lester Tribute. "Wait a minute," he interjected. "There's something in the *Los*

Ricardo Montalban in
Return to Fantasy Island (1977).

Angeles Times about that." He showed me a half-page ad in the paper. Reading it stunned me. I had no idea this was going to be such an enormous event. Ticket sales benefiting the Los Angeles Music Center were going for $50–250, a great deal of money in 1985. The early estimate of funds raised was $150,000. The actual show brought even more. Something like terror fought with elation inside me. Elation won, and that night my husband and I had one of the greatest nights of our lives.

A week later found me at the Music Center, dressed like a dancer in black tights, a cut-up T-shirt, and my old jazz dance shoes with metal taps. Entering through the stage entrance was a rare thrill. The large rehearsal hall had a few chairs scattered about, a piano player, Aida, and seven other dancers, all seasoned professionals who appeared to know each other. Aida made quick introductions and appointed the dance captain, who assists the choreographer in any dance group context. She is also the dancers' go-to person for help and advice. With formalities out of the way, our first rehearsal began. Everything went fine at first, and I was able to quickly pick up the routine.

Then the routine was sped up. Five, six, seven, eight. Front cross, double back, single tap, turn and slide. Then came the commands. "Watch the spacing, make it bigger, cover the stage." Everything was getting faster and louder. I had been told in my earlier dance career that I was an intellectual dancer, not an intuitive one. It made picking up routines more difficult for me. Before I knew it, my mind and legs were going in different directions. Mercifully, lunch was finally called.

Aida approached me as I sat by myself trying to catch my breath and eat my sandwich at the same time. Without a trace of warmth, she said, "You're falling behind. Try and keep up. Watch the girl in front of you." Then she abruptly walked off.

Thank God the afternoon was short, and we were dismissed for the day. Day two's call was for the afternoon, giving me time to practice at home. Feeling somewhat confident that day, I arrived at rehearsal, only to be told there was a second routine to be learned. There I was, in the same predicament as the day before, crossing front instead of back, going left instead of right, etc. Making matters worse, one of the dancers suggested that we do a double tap and a spin toward the end of the number.

"Good. Put it in, but don't lose the timing," Aida ordered.

Well, I never was very good at tap dancing, and after so many years my body couldn't remember how to double tap and spin at the same time. After a long and embarrassing reprimand from Aida, I assured her I would work on it at home and that it would be fine by tomorrow's run-through and dress rehearsal. The discussion closed, and Aida called a fifteen-minute break.

Shattered in body and soul, I slunk off to the water fountain in the hall. Approaching it at the same time was a tall, elegant man, casually but stylishly dressed. Favoring me with a dazzling smile, he said, "After you." It was Ricardo Montalban, taking a break from rehearsing on the main stage with the other celebrities appearing in the Lester tribute.

"Thank you," I responded, hesitantly leaning in to get a drink.

"Are you one of the dancers?" he asked, in that magnetic voice of his.

"Well, at least for the moment I am."

"What do you mean, for the moment?"

"I used to be a dancer in a past life, but now I just act. Keeping up with these professional dancers is proving to be almost impossible. I don't know why I was hired."

"Maybe it's because you're lovely, but I know what you mean. My dancing days are long gone, too. Don't worry, you'll be fine." With that, he gave me an encouraging pat on the shoulder and returned to the main stage.

I went back to my group for a few more run-throughs, none of which went well for me, and then we all went home. "Get some rest. Tomorrow is showtime," Aida called out.

Showtime! The third and final day. First, there was a run-through with the entire cast, including celebrities, then a dress rehearsal, and finally the big event. Most of the celebrities appearing in the show, including Mary Martin, Carol Channing, Patricia Morrison, Robert Morse, John Raitt, Ricardo Montalban, and many others, were seated in the orchestra section of the Dorothy Chandler Pavilion watching the run-through and jumping onstage when their musical number was scheduled. We dancers were offstage and "magically" appeared during scene changes or when one of the stars needed us to enhance their performance.

Our first routine was a tough one, and I messed up. Aida yelled, "Stop! Sandra, pay attention! You *do* know your right foot from your left, don't you? Let's do it again." We did, and I messed up again, and Aida yelled again. We did it a third time, and I botched it a third time. Aida now shouted at the top of her lungs, "Sandra! Get it right or get out! This show can do without you!" I felt so humiliated, I didn't know whether to cry or to run.

Suddenly, there came a loud, clear, familiar male voice from the orchestra section, "Some of us no longer dance, we act!" All eyes turned to Ricardo Montalban. He didn't get up, just sat with his legs draped over the seat in front of him, coolly staring at Aida as if daring her to continue her tirade. A long, uncomfortable moment of silence ensued. Finally, the captain of our dance group stepped forward and broke the tension. "It's okay, Aida. I'm sure it's a simple adjustment. I'll work with Sandra, and she'll be fine." I was. (I still have the photos.)

That opening night proved to be a fantastic experience for performers and capacity audience alike. The stellar reviews next day attested to this. I will only describe one of the musical performances, as this story is about a gentleman who wouldn't tolerate the public humiliation of another human being, much less a fellow artist. Ricardo Montalban performed the song "A Puzzlement" from the *The King and I*. He talked his way through it with an affecting emotional intensity. He moved, but he didn't dance, he acted. He passed by me on his way offstage, and I gave him a heartfelt thumbs-up. He cocked his head the way he often did in his films, gave me a big wink, and went backstage.

The wrap party in the Pavilion's Founders Room was filled with happy and excited performers, journalists, and, of course, an open bar and great food. As I was leaving, I waved at my gentleman knight, who favored me with that inimitable smile and a friendly wave in return.

I never danced professionally again, but I closed out my dance career center stage with a standing ovation, surrounded by the best of that era's musical entertainers at the Dorothy Chandler Pavilion.

A year later, while attending a performance at the Music Center, who did I spot but Ricardo Montalban in the lobby, surrounded by a group of people. Hesitating but a moment, I walked over and tapped him on the shoulder. He turned and gave me a blank look, recognition temporarily eluding him. I smiled and said, "Some of us no longer dance, we act."

He threw back his head, flashed that incredible smile, and said, "That was a memorable night, and you made it through like a star!" We said our adios and went our separate ways to our reserved seats.

I never saw or met him again, but I will always remember his chivalry, his smile, and that wink. Some men are worth remembering, none more so than Ricardo Montalban.

PAUL NEWMAN

1925–2008

**The most famous blue eyes in movie history. They flashed,
stared at me, then smiled. How lucky can a gal get?**

*(Paul Newman was a legendary screen icon from the 1950s through
the 1990s. He was nominated for nine Academy Awards, including
for* Cat on a Hot Tin Roof *(1958),* The Hustler *(1961),* Cool Hand
Luke *(1967),* Butch Cassidy and the Sundance Kid *(1969),* The
Sting *(1973),* The Verdict *(1982), and several others. He won the
Oscar for best actor for* The Color of Money *(1986). He was nominated for a Tony Award in 2003 for* Our Town. *He also produced
and directed the film* Rachel, Rachel *(1968), for which he won a
Golden Globe award for directing. He was equally known for his
philanthropic endeavors and successful business ventures, as well as
his sense of humor, and, yes, his race car driving. He finished second
in the 24 Hours of Le Mans endurance race in 1979.)*

Parking with Paul

It was a beautiful sunny day in Southern California in the early
1970s as my red Dodge convertible sped me from West Hollywood to Hunter's Books in Beverly Hills in search of reading
material on film and theater. Newly arrived in Hollywood, I
knew nothing about the workings of the Dream Factory, and was
diligently researching all of its angels and devils.

The bookstore was located on Little Santa Monica Boulevard, and I turned into the commercial parking lot behind the store. There was free head-in parking, with two side-by-side spaces available from which to choose. Spotting a small silver car close behind in my rearview mirror, I did the polite thing and parked in the furthest spot, leaving the space on the right open for the other driver.

As I switched off the ignition, I felt a sharp bump on my right rear fender. That silver compact had clipped my right tail end. Yeah, just smacked it! My mind went into furious overdrive. *I had left the driver plenty of room. How could he be so stupid? Was this some Beverly Hills elitist?*

By now, the man driving the car had pulled into the vacant spot, turned off his engine, and rolled down his tinted window. In disbelief, I leaned across my front seat and yelled at him from the passenger window, "Been driving long?"

The guy jerked his head to look at me, noticeably taken aback. I had a fleeting sensation that I somehow knew him, but that didn't stop me from jumping out of my car to inspect the damage he'd inflicted on my poor little red convertible. The culprit was already out of his car and hunkered down studying my rear-end fender.

"Well?" I challenged him.

"Just a scrape. Sorry!" he answered as he stood up.

"Oh!" was all I could say. Why was I, normally never at a loss for words, so tongue-tied? Then it dawned on me, because standing in front of me, famous blue eyes sparkling, dressed in, of all things, a silver jumpsuit, was Paul Newman.

For one of the few times in my life, I was speechless, and could only stare at him. After what seemed like minutes, but was probably only seconds, he said, somewhat cavalierly, "I'll certainly pay

Paul Newman in the driver's seat in the
television special *Once Upon a Wheel* (1971).

for the damage. My business manager will take care of it. Here,
I'll get you his card."

My voice, uncontrollably a tad higher than normal, finally
returned. "No, no, no! That's not necessary. It's only a scratch."

"It was my reckless driving and/or bad parking. I insist," he
countered.

"No, it's alright. It really is. The scratch was probably there
before you hit me."

"I doubt it," he answered, clearly surprised by my retort.

Now my nerves really jangled. My hair needed combing, I
had forgotten to put lipstick on, and here I was talking to Paul
Newman, still Hollywood's reigning heartthrob. He took a step
forward and asked with a smile, "I *would* like to take care of it.
Why won't you let me?"

"Well, because, because . . . you're *Paul Newman*!"

"Yeah, I know that!" he answered with an amused smirk.

"Look, it's okay. It really is," I responded.

"No, it really isn't," he said.

"Yes, it is. Now, *please* go away," I pleaded.

The perfect gentleman, he tried not to laugh, though his blue eyes twinkled. "Why?"

"Because you're making me terribly nervous."

"Oh, because I'm Paul Newman?"

"Yes!"

"Well, okay. Can't change that! Where are you going?"

"To Hunter's Books."

"So am I. Mind if I walk with you?"

"Yeah, I guess that's okay."

Down the street and around the corner to Hunter's Books together we went, Butch Cassidy and a still-nervous Sandra de Bruin. At first, we didn't talk as we walked. Finally, he said, "You know, I really *have* been driving a long time. In fact, I'm considered one of the top race car drivers around."

"Well, I don't know if I'd bet on you, but that's nice."

"Is this a lesson in humility?"

"Not really. Let's just forget the whole thing. Okay?"

"Okay, if you insist."

Minutes later, we reached Hunter's, where we parted. I made my way to the theatrical section. Mr. Newman seemed to disappear. After picking out the books I wanted, I approached the cashier with my checkbook in hand. (In those days, before credit cards were widely accepted, you paid with cash, check, or a charge account.) "How much do I owe you?" I asked.

The clerk smiled and said, "Mr. Newman has taken care of it. And he said to pick out whatever else you want."

Momentarily stunned, I thanked her profusely, asked her to thank Mr. Newman for me, picked out another book on Hollywood, and returned to my car. Mr. Cool Hand Luke's car was gone. I drove home, promptly broke out my red nail polish, and in tiny print wrote on the scratched fender, "PN did this."

The story traveled among my friends. Some laughed, some were awed, and a few asked why I hadn't sued him. The last option never occurred to me.

Years went by, maybe two, maybe four. Paul Newman had partnered with some friends in two deluxe hamburger restaurants in Los Angeles called Hamptons. There was one in Hollywood and one on Ventura Boulevard in the San Fernando Valley near Studio City. They were reasonably priced, casual, and very popular showbiz joints. Actors and below-the-line crew members filled the wooden tables every night. You ordered your hamburger and salad, paid for it, and a waitress brought your order to your assigned table.

By now, my career had sort of taken off, and I was far more sophisticated and confident about the workings of Hollywood. I had met some stars and been to awards shows. Nobody really intimidated me.

One night, a few friends and I went to the Hampton's near Studio City for dinner. We ordered our hamburgers and sauntered towards our table. One of the servers whispered that Paul Newman was there. I surreptitiously glanced around as we made our way to our table. Sure enough, surrounded by a few friends, was the man himself. Without a moment's hesitation, I strode to his table, tapped him on the shoulder—much to the consternation of his companions—and said, "Been driving long?"

Mr. Blue Eyes froze for a moment, then jumped up, flashed a big grin, and exclaimed, "You! One of the greatest lines I've ever had thrown at me! How are you? How is your car? How is your career going?"

I thought for a moment he was going to hug me, but he somehow resisted the urge. We joked and laughed for a few minutes, almost like old friends. Finally, in a replay of the Hunter's Books incident, he insisted on paying for my dinner. I cut him off, explaining that it was already paid for, but maybe next time. We chatted a bit more about this, that, and his illustrious career, then went our separate ways.

Unfortunately, I never met him again, but to this day I often dream about a man in a silver jumpsuit with beautiful blue sparkling eyes looking down at my shiny, scratched, black self-autographed fender.

DOLLY PARTON

1946–

Five-feet-none, homespun and can't be outdone. That's Dolly Parton. One can watch her sing and act, or hang out with her "nine to five," and I had the good fortune to do just that.

(Dolly Parton needs no introduction. She is as renowned today as she was in the 1970s. She actually began her career as a singer/ songwriter in the late 1960s at the Grand Ole Opry in Nashville, but soon branched out on her own. Many of her numerous hit songs have garnered Grammy and Country Music awards. She even received an Oscar nomination for writing the title song for Nine to Five *(1980), in which she made her film debut. Dolly followed that with such successful films as* Rhinestone *(1984) and* Steel Magnolias *(1989), plus dozens of theatrical and television films. Her award-winning songs include "Jolene," "I Will Always Love You," "Here You Come Again," and "Nine to Five." In between, she has done numerous television specials, often with megastars like Kenny Rogers (her great and good friend) and other country and cross-over artists. Her most famous quote is: "My music is what took me everywhere I've been and everywhere I will go. It's my greatest love.")*

In the Loop with Dolly

In the mid-1980s, I was part of The Looping Group run by Barbara Harris. Not Broadway's Barbara Harris, but a talented, dynamite lady whose theatrical name is Barbara Iley. Looping is not to be confused with dubbing, wherein an actor actually voices another actor. Looping is providing background voices that are vaguely heard in crowd scenes, restaurants, or on the street when a film's main characters are talking or engaged in romantic byplay or a heroic endeavor. As loopers, we are given in advance the name of the project, where it takes place, the year it occurs, and other pertinent information so that our muffled conversations fit in with the time and place of the story. This always requires a bit of research. For example, if a film is set in France in 1940, we have to brush up on what happened in the 1940s, hopefully mix in some French, and keep our conversations about that time in history.

In 1984, the Looping Group was hired to do the looping on the film *Rhinestone*, starring Sylvester Stallone and Dolly Parton. One scene took place in a rundown Italian bar (trattoria) in New York City. Since I speak Italian—albeit a broken Italian, but nonetheless Italian—I was called in to work. My day started off just murmuring different Italian phrases and mixing in with other loopers performing background barroom conversations in English and Italian. Also in the scene was a tipsy female piano singer perched upon a dusty stage, lustily belting out popular Italian and American songs.

Just before the lunch break, Barbara Harris approached me and said, "The director wants you to loop in an Italian song for that piano singer. When they shot this scene, she did 'Swanee River,' and he wants to change it to the Italian song 'Funiculi, Funicula.'"*

I stood paralyzed for a moment. I can't carry a tune or even sing a note. My friends delight in ridiculing me about this talent I don't possess. But since Barbara prided herself on having

Musical legend Dolly Parton.

the most talented and versatile loopers in town, I wasn't about to admit this limitation. I smiled my best innocent smile, and said, "Oh, I'm sorry, I don't know the lyrics to that song."

"Don't worry," Barbara replied. "The director thought you might not know them all, so he's already sent someone out to get them. We'll do it after the lunch break."

I felt a panic attack coming on. This couldn't be happening to me, but what could I do or say? Both Barbara and the director, Bob Clark of *A Christmas Story* (1983) fame, wanted "Funiculi, Funicula" sung by *me*, dammit, the only female cast member who they *thought* was fluent in Italian.

It seemed like the longest lunch break I can remember. There was free food, but I couldn't eat a bite. A million thoughts ran through my head, none of them reassuring. Should I tell them I can't sing a note? Should I run out the door? Should I feign sick, or should I just kill myself?

Just to compound my anxiety, after the lunch break there was a buzz around the set that Dolly Parton had dropped in to see how the looping was going. There she was, wearing jeans and a loose shirt, no makeup, and no hair extensions, chatting away with everyone in her wonderful southern drawl, totally at ease as if she was just one of the cast or crew.

My moment came. I was seated in the middle of the set, the center of everyone's undivided attention, with a microphone and the lyrics to "Funiculi, Funicula" on a stand in front of me. The taped music started . . . and so did I. At first, I stumbled, so we started again. This time, I got through it, and I got through it again, and again, and again.

Then, mercifully, I heard, "Cut! That's fine, Sandra. Thank you!"

I stood up and started to walk back to where the other loopers were hanging out, when suddenly Dolly Parton rushed up to me and said, "That was amazing! *How* did you do it?"

Stunned, I could only reply, "What do you mean, 'How did I do it?'"

"You didn't hit *one note*. Not once!"

For a split-second I thought she was being sarcastic, but then I realized she was paying me an extraordinary compliment. Of course, to her a feat of such musical incompetence was impossible. All I could blurt out was, "Well, thank you. But remember, the singer is supposed to be quite drunk, and drunks never sing on key. I thought that's the way I should do it."

Dolly stared back at me, somewhat awed. "That's incredible. I would have figured out she was drunk, but I never could have sung it totally off-key. You must be quite an actress. You go, gal!" With that, she walked away, giving me a thumbs-up and a huge smile.

After that, everyone, including Barbara, rushed up to congratulate me. Bob Clark even played it back so everyone could hear it again as I tried to smile through my embarrassment.

The day finally ended, and the paycheck came in. To this day, I can't hear that song without cringing. Several months later, I saw the final cut of *Rhinestone*, and when that barroom scene appeared and I heard my drunken rendition of this classic Italian song—which seemed to fill the entire theatre—my heart became a bongo drum, and I could feel the flush in my cheeks rush all the way down to my feet. Then I remembered Dolly Parton's warm compliments and encouragement. What the heck, I'll take kudos in whatever form they arrive, and this one arrived from the best of the best.

*[Note: For post-1980s generations "Funiculi, Funicula" is a traditional Italian song written in 1880 to celebrate the opening of the first funicular railway on Mount Vesuvius. It quickly became a worldwide success, and has been used to enliven countless films.]

ELVIS PRESLEY

1935–1977

I liked Elvis Presley. I enjoyed his music. I danced to his rock 'n' roll. However, I was never a rabid fan until. . . .

(When you say the phrase "the King of Rock 'n' Roll," everyone knows, even decades after his passing, that you're talking about Elvis Presley, who remains one of the preeminent cultural icons of the 20th century. He made his first tentative recordings in 1953, honed his craft over the next two years, and struck gold in 1956 with "Heartbreak Hotel." The rest, as they say, is history. Elvis' musical accomplishments alone are awe-inspiring. He was inducted into five music halls of fame: Rock 'n' Roll, Country, Gospel, Rockabilly, and R&B. More than 2.5 billion of his records have sold worldwide, not to mention having fifty-three Top 40 albums on the Billboard Top 200 charts. Elvis was king at the box office, too, with a string of massively popular films throughout the late 1950s and 1960s. For all his success, Elvis retained a basic humility and a down-to-earth perspective on fame, saying, "If you let your head get too big, it'll break your neck." His charitable activities are almost as legendary as his celebrity. Making him even more a "man for the people" was his sensitive concern for the problems of others and his ability to easily mix with people from all walks of life. The man rocked in every way.)

A Life-Changing Cup of Coffee with Elvis

Las Vegas in the early 1970s was still the classic old Las Vegas, often referred to as Sin City. It was filled with celebrities leisurely milling around and brilliant onstage performances by such luminaries as Sammy Davis Jr., Frank Sinatra, Juliet Prowse, Dean Martin, and, of course, Elvis Presley. The slot machines paid out real money in coins. Folks cheered as the winning jangle of coins spilling out of the machines rang out through the casinos. Included in Sin City's attractions were lavish shows, high-end rollers, gorgeous showgirls, ethnic gangsters, and money that seemed to grow on trees. It was America's wanna-be Monte Carlo. At that time, it was definitely not a place for family gatherings or class reunions. It was, however, a place where an attractive girl could make a pile of money working as a dancer, a showgirl, or even a waitress. Yes, some gals worked at less-traditional occupations. Dealers made the best money, but that required lengthy schooling, so it wasn't an obvious choice for a gal looking for a quick, temporary, well-paying job.

My career was just starting to take off, but I was constantly scrambling to make ends meet. A casual friend of mine named Sharon—a beautiful, fun-loving blond I met in the same dance class where I encountered Cher—had moved to Las Vegas and was now making good money as a topless showgirl at the Sands. We kept in touch, and during one of our phone calls she suggested I come stay for a couple of months and get a job doing almost anything in one of the renowned casinos. I could bank some money and then return to Los Angeles and comfortably continue my pursuit of an acting career. I was a little hesitant, but

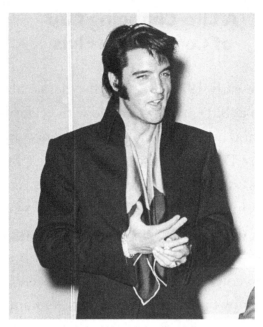

The King, Elvis Presley,
International Hotel, Las Vegas, 1969.

when Sharon assured me that this was a tried-and-true strategy,
I put aside my reservations and flew out there to initiate my Sin
City job search.

Sharon arranged for me to stay at a cheap local motel, since
her place was uncomfortably small and crowded with small children and relatives. We filled the day I arrived with shopping and
sightseeing. That evening, Sharon dropped me back at my motel
and went on to do her early show. She left me a free pass to her
ten o'clock show, telling me to dress to the nines and to meet her
afterward. "We'll party," she promised.

Sharon was in a considerable state of excitement when I
met her after her late show. "Elvis is in town," she breathlessly
exclaimed, "and he's invited us to join him at Caesars Palace in
the baccarat room. Come on!"

"What?"

"Oh, didn't I tell you that I know Elvis? *Weeelll*, whenever he's in town we spend the evening together." Call me naïve, but I just stared at her, speechless.

Sharon was obviously amused by my innocence and couldn't resist adding the kicker, purring, "He has red silk pajamas."

There was no comeback to that, so we piled into her car and drove off down the fabled strip to Caesars.

Upon arrival, we were escorted to a large private room complete with a baccarat table, roulette wheel, one slot machine, and a bar with a scantily dressed waitress serving drinks. Off to one side, like extras in a classic Hollywood movie about Las Vegas, sat a few people at small tables engrossed in serious private conversations.

Holding court at the baccarat table, surrounded by his doting entourage, was the king himself, Elvis Aaron Presley. Casually dressed, with that legendary lock of jet-black hair falling carelessly above one of his blue eyes, he interrupted his playing to warmly greet Sharon and politely nod at me as we were introduced. I'd seen him in films, of course, but was unprepared for the force of his charisma in person. Elvis resumed his gambling and Sharon hung out next to him, so I shuffled around in the background for what seemed like an eternity. Suddenly, a pudgy, unattractive man snaked his arm around my waist and an unctuous voice said, "Can I get you a drink, honey?" It was none other than Colonel Tom Parker, Elvis' colorful, controversial, unscrupulous, and sleazy manager.

"No thank you," I said, somewhat icily. "I don't drink alcohol."

"How does a Shirley Temple sound?" he countered with a smirk.

"I'm fine, thank you. I'm just here visiting Sharon."

"Well, now, how about I stake you for some chips and you can play roulette or the slots?" he continued, totally ignoring my obvious disinterest while drawing me in tighter against him.

That did it. Pulling away from him, I said, loud enough for everyone in the room to hear, "If you're asking whether or not I need subsidizing, I *don't!*"

A howl went up from the baccarat table. Several of the men jeered the Colonel: "Ha-ha! That'll teach you." "You can't win them all." "You're not her type."

I wanted to disappear, even though I'd done nothing but stand up for myself against a smug, overbearing lecher. But Parker was rich and powerful, and I was not. For a long, uncomfortable moment, I was the center of unwanted attention.

Then Elvis walked over to me, and with a warm smile said, "Can I at least get you a cup of coffee?"

Pausing only briefly, I said, "Yes, that would be . . . that would be nice." I glanced at Sharon, who nodded approvingly. Elvis and I moved to one of the side tables and took a seat. A cup of coffee magically appeared. For a moment or two, neither one of us spoke. Elvis looked at me, and I looked down. I didn't know what to say or do. Finally, he broke the silence. "What are you doing in Vegas?"

"I'm visiting Sharon. I'm going to look for a job as a dancer or maybe a waitress. I've heard the money is good here."

"What do you do? Where are you from?" he questioned in that famous deep voice.

(I honestly can't remember verbatim how the rest of conversation went, but it was pretty close to the following.) "I'm from Los Angeles, and I'm an actress. But the bank and I are always running neck and neck. From what I've read, you started out with a similar problem, so you know how it is. A six-month gig in Las Vegas would enable me to put away enough money to pursue my career with less money problems."

Elvis nodded and smiled. "Yeah, it's tough getting started." He spoke in a sympathetic and understanding way. Not once did he mention himself, his career, his public or private life. He seemed interested only in me, my career, my ambitions. He appeared in no hurry to leave. It was comforting, and flattering, but after a quarter of an hour I began to feel uneasy. There I was, monopolizing the King of Rock 'n' Roll, who was also Sharon's date. I thanked him for his time and made some excuse that I had to go back to my motel and get ready for the next day's job hunt. We ended our coffee break, Elvis returned to Sharon and the baccarat table, and I bid goodnight to everyone (excluding the "Colonel") and took a taxi back to my motel.

As I finished dressing the next morning, there came a knock on my door. I opened it to find a nicely dressed middle-aged man standing in the hallway with an envelope in his hand. I immediately recognized him as part of Elvis' entourage. Introducing himself, he said, "Mr. Presley sent me here to take you to the airport so you can return to Los Angeles. He said to tell you: 'You don't belong in Vegas.'" Handing me the envelope, he continued, "Here's your ticket."

I stood there in shock, just staring at him. But my inner self knew that Elvis was right. I *didn't* belong in Vegas. Last night had made it quite clear. After a pause, I stammered, "I have to take care of the motel bill."

"I'll take care of it while you pack up. Get your stuff together. We'll leave in ten minutes." He turned and headed toward the motel office.

Three hours later, I was safely back home in my West Hollywood bungalow. As I lay in bed that night, I went over all that had transpired during the last forty-eight hours. The bottom line: a terrible mistake had been avoided, thanks to a caring megastar. It didn't dawn on me until the next day that I, Sandra de Bruin, had spent fifteen private special minutes with Elvis Presley. I often wondered, and still do, why he took such an interest in me. Perhaps my innocent defiance, dark hair, and green eyes reminded him of Priscilla, his young wife and only real love.

The next day, I sat down and wrote Elvis a thank you note. I sent it to Graceland in Memphis, Tennessee, but I never heard back. Some things are best left just the way they are. Rock on, Elvis. You are missed.

JASON ROBARDS

1922–2000

**It's called charisma. Some people have it, some people don't.
Jason Robards had it both onscreen and in his everyday life.**

*(Jason Robards was a legendary American stage and film actor,
one of the few to receive the Triple Crown of Acting: two Academy Awards, one for* All the President's Men *(1976) and the
other for* Julia *(1977); a Tony Award for* The Disenchanted *in
1959; and an Emmy Award for* Inherit the Wind *in 1988. He
received numerous other nominations for Tonys and Oscars
during his career, as well as the Kennedy Center Honors Ribbon.
Robards first gained attention on Broadway in Eugene O'Neill's*
Long Day's Journey into Night *(1956), but shot to fame starring in the stage version of* A Thousand Clowns *in 1963 and
the film version in 1965. He never stopped working in either
medium. Like many in his profession, his personal life had its
dark moments. He married Lauren Bacall in 1961, but she
divorced him in 1969 due to his alcoholism. Years later, following a car accident, he got himself under control, and became an
advocate for drinking responsibly.)*

I Got the Drink and
the "Thump, Thump!"

In the summer of 1968, I took temporarily leave of Hollywood
and returned to New York City for a summer acting semester

with Sanford Meisner at the Neighborhood Playhouse. Of course, I stayed with my folks at our family apartment located between Central Park West and Columbus Avenue, just two blocks north of the high-end, well-known Dakota Apartments. (Think John Lennon, Yoko Ono, Humphrey Bogart, Lauren Bacall, and Jason Robards.) Our apartment was on the second floor. A small section of it was directly above Paddy Jordan's, the local pub (think *Cheers* in real life). During the thirty odd years my parents lived there, Dad would occasionally drop in to Jordan's for a drink or to watch a game, while Mom would handle various domestic problems that arose from the pub, such as plumbing and New York cockroaches. We were all on friendly terms (except with the cockroaches).

Mom's mother, Hazel, lived on the sixth floor in a studio apartment. She was simply Hazel to everyone and Aunt Hazel to me, as she never wanted to be called Grandma. Aunt Hazel was a character, an eccentric with rolled-down stockings and a dyed-red clump of old lady hair. She was as nuts as my mother was normal. (Never figured out how that happened.) Hazel's two loves were astrology and the racetrack. Early every morning, she would venture out to the newsstand on the corner of 72nd street and Columbus Avenue to pick up the racing form. Later in the day, she would go place her two-dollar bet at the local book-maker. Occasionally, she won.

One morning, as I was getting ready to leave for my class, my mother received a phone call. All I heard was, "What? I'll be right down!" Then, "Sandra! Go down to Paddy Jordan's and get Hazel."

"What are you talking about?" I asked.

"Hazel is drunk at the bar with Jason Robards. I'm not dressed, so you go," she answered, visibly upset.

Jason Robards, from *All the President's Men* (1976).

"Jason Robards? You've got to be kidding."

"Just go, Sandra. Details later, and don't come back without her!" she snapped as she disappeared into her bedroom to throw some clothes on.

It's not every day one is called upon to retrieve a drunken relative from a drunken celebrity. Dutiful daughter that I was, I grabbed my purse, ran down the stairs, rushed around the corner, and burst into the den of iniquity called Paddy Jordan's. Sure enough, seated at the end of the bar was Aunt Hazel and . . . Jason Robards, in the flesh. They were deep in animated and intense conversation, like two people who have known each other for years—and obviously drunk out of their minds. Fortunately, they were the sole patrons in the pub. As I approached the early morning inebriates, Aunt Hazel looked up and recognized me. "Sandra!" she yelped with drunken excitement.

"Sandra! Come meet Jason Robards. He can help you with your acting career."

At that, the famous Jason Robards stood up on cue and graciously offered me his seat. Always a gentleman, drunk or sober. Although Hazel and Jason were plastered, we managed after a fashion to fulfill the obligatory social ritual of "Nice to meet you. Thank you. Nice to meet *you*." I then turned to Hazel and asked, "What *are* you doing here?"

"*Wellll*," she began, slurring her words slightly. "I was at the newsstand buying my racing form, when Mr. *Robards* walked by. I went up to him and told him what a *brilliant* actor he is, but that he should *really* give up drinking. It's giving him a *bad reputation*! He agreed to talk about it, and suggested we come here to discuss it. So, *here* we are!" She capped this dubious recitation with a florid gesture.

I stared dumbfounded at my Aunt Hazel. Several awkward moments of silence reigned, when suddenly: "Can I buy you a drink?" blurted the famous thespian Jason Robards.

"No! Thank you!" I answered, a little too forcefully. I don't recall if I clearly registered the fact that Jason Robards had just offered to buy me a drink, and what motivation or intent might lay behind that offer, conscious or unconscious.

Instead, I faced Aunt Hazel. "Hazel, I'm sure Mr. Robards can take care of his own life. Now, say goodbye and let's go home."

But our absurd little comedy hadn't quite reached its conclusion. Confusion intervened in the matter of the bill, which the gallant Mr. Robards insisted upon paying. Eventually, we all somehow managed to stumble/walk out the door. As if my mortification needed nourishment, Hazel insisted upon having the last word. Turning to Mr. Robards, she said, "Remember what

I *said*: Watch your *drinking*, and I'll do your astrological chart, which will tell you what to expect in your life."

"Thank you. I'm looking forward to that." With that, Jason Robards blew Hazel a boozy kiss, turned, and staggered back toward the Dakota and the apartment he shared with his wife, the iconic and beautiful Lauren Bacall. They were divorced soon after.

That evening, I regaled my father with the events of the morning. He did his best to control his laughter, given that my Mom was still furious and had banished Aunt Hazel to her own studio apartment.

A month later, my semester at the Neighborhood Playhouse came to an end, and I returned to Hollywood. Studying under Sanford Meisner had made me a better actress and looked good on my resume. I began in earnest my professional career as a working actor.

About ten years later, I joined some friends for dinner at a small, chic restaurant on Melrose Avenue. As the server took our drinks order, I heard a distinct, deep, sexy, *familiar* voice emanating from a table across the room. It took me but a moment to realize that the voice belonged to Jason Robards. He had just won the Best Supporting Actor Academy Award for *All the President's Men* (1976), a film about the Watergate scandal. (I loved that film. Almost everyone did. Well, maybe some Republicans didn't.) One moment that stuck with me was the two-finger "thump-thump" that Robards' character, *Washington Post* Editor-in-Chief Ben Bradlee, tapped on a newsroom desk after green-lighting the key story by reporters Bob Woodward and Carl Bernstein. My friends didn't remember the gesture, so I stood up and, in my best dramatic style, acted it out for them.

A half-hour later, Jason Robards and his friends finished their dinner and passed our table as they made their exit. He suddenly paused, peered closely at me, lifted his eyebrows, and casually did his two-finger "thump-thump" on our table. I threw my head back and laughed. He smiled back at me and went on his way.

It's amazing how a good actor can do such a simple thing and make it indelible in the minds of an audience. Jason Robards was an artist at it.

CLIFF ROBERTSON

1923–2011

Throughout my career, I've enjoyed a number of repeat chance meetings with various Hollywood luminaries, perhaps none so memorable as my close encounters of the Cliff Robertson kind.

(Every film generation boasts a handful of actor's actors, leading men and women whose work is exceptional yet unaffected in ways that fellow performers recognize. Cliff Robertson was such a paradigm during a sparkling career that spanned five-plus decades. He did acclaimed work in film and television early in his career, having come from a strong stage background. In 1963, he played Navy lieutenant John F. Kennedy in the World War II film PT 109, *which brought him semi-stardom. He gave indelible performances in memorable-yet-overlooked films throughout the rest of the decade, including* Underworld U.S.A. *(1961),* Sunday in New York *(1963),* The Best Man *(1964), and* Masquerade *(1965). Yet major stardom eluded him until 1968, when he played an intellectually disabled adult who undergoes an experiment that temporarily imbues him with a super-intellect. That film was* Charly, *and it won him a much-deserved Oscar. In 1970, however, his career came to a standstill when he exposed Columbia Picture's studio head, David Begelman, of embezzling money through forged actors' checks. Hollywood didn't thank Cliff. The studios stood behind their executives, no matter how corrupt, and Cliff was blacklisted for several years. (David McClintick's 1982 book*

Indecent Exposure *details the entire sordid story.) After a year or so, Cliff's career once again took an uphill turn in such high-profile films as* Three Days of the Condor *(1975),* Obsession *(1976),* Midway *(1976), and* Return to Earth *(1976), the television movie about Buzz Aldrin, the second astronaut to walk on the moon, which detailed his subsequent mental breakdown as his career and marriage disintegrated. Towards the end of Cliff's career, he appeared in the first three* Spider-Man *films, and also became active in Screen Actors Guild politics.)*

Driving Round and Round with Cliff

In 1976, I had the good fortune to be cast as Buzz Aldrin's Air Force secretary in *Return to Earth*. The shoot date was an "on or about," meaning sometime in a week or so, giving me an opportunity to work on other shows.

The timing was right, as Lady Luck smiled on me and I was cast on the mystery/comedy TV series *Ellery Queen* (1975–1976). Dina Merrill, the beautiful New York socialite turned actor, then married to Cliff, was the guest star. The breakdown for my character was: "an inept secretary in a lawyer's outer office." The scene opened with me filing my nails when Dina, accompanied by her male assistant, entered and announced herself at my desk. I was to buzz my boss that she had arrived, then jump up and escort her to his office. When I bounced up, I accidently knocked over my pencil holder, sending pens and pencils all over the floor at her feet. I babbled an incoherent apology as her male assistant began picking up the pencils. This sent the crew and some onlookers (including Cliff, to my surprise) into laugher.

The director, however, was not amused, and irritably yelled, "Cut! Let's go again. Sandra, try not to knock over the pencils this time."

Encouraged by the laughs, and not wanting to acknowledge it was a clumsy accident, I countered, "Well, the character description says she's inept. I thought it would be funny."

There was a pause while the director gave this some thought. "Okay, go with it. But for the record, the description says inept, not clumsy." The director always has to have the last word, as well he should.

We did one or two more takes, including close-ups, then moved into the lawyer's office, where I made introductions. As I turned to leave, I suddenly remembered the hilarious scene in *Day for Night* (1973) in which the talented Italian actress Valentina Cortese kept opening or colliding with the wrong door. With that in mind, I deliberately walked smack into the open office door. Dina did a marvelous "I don't believe her" reaction, rolling her eyes upward. I muttered something and exited tentatively, closing the door behind me. Everyone stifled a laugh. The director yelled, "Cut! Good! Like it. Let's do it again." (Ingrid Bergman in her Academy Award acceptance speech in 1974 for Best Supporting Actress said that the award should have gone to Cortese.)

We performed the scene a few more times before moving back to my outer office set to film Dina and her assistant making their exit. That was it for the day. After saying farewell and thank you to all, I gathered my things from my trailer and started the long walk to my car on the Universal Studios back lot. Not far from the sound stage, a nondescript car pulled up beside me and a male voice called out, "Can I give you a lift to your car?"

Cliff Robertson, a true gentleman.

Without looking, I gratefully replied, "That would be great." (This was common practice on the studio lot, so I didn't hesitate about accepting.) After getting myself, my wardrobe, and other stuff situated in the passenger seat, I turned to look at the driver. It was Cliff Robertson.

Not knowing what to say, I blurted out, "Oh, it's you!"

He laughed and complimented me on my performance, which I graciously accepted. We chatted briefly about *Charly* (which he was very proud of), then I asked him how Dina was going to get home. He grinned. "They have a limo for her."

We arrived at my car all too soon. As I opened my door to exit, I thanked him for the lift and added, "By the way, next week I'm playing your military secretary in *Return to Earth*. I'm really honored to work with you."

Without missing a beat, he said, "Whoa. Good casting. Now you are the official family secretary. See you next week. Drive carefully." Off he went.

Driving home, I felt like I had just drunk a bottle of the best wine. What a great day and what a week. What a week the next week would be: working with Cliff Robertson.

I arrived at CBS on the designated filming day at the crack of dawn, and joined several of the male cast members in a van that took us to Edwards Air Force Base thirty miles north of Los Angeles. Everyone was relatively subdued, running their lines alone or with each other, but subdued vanished upon arrival, when everything went amuck. Trailers weren't set up, the Honey Wagon didn't arrive to serve breakfast, wardrobe had the wrong medals for the Air Force uniforms, and locations for the different shots were scattered all over the base.

Eventually, however, things settled down, and the first shot was set up. This was a boardroom scene involving most of the male actors I had ridden up with from Los Angeles. As the camera rolled, the main character in the scene, a well-respected actor, froze. Director/producer Jud Taylor started over. The actor froze again, and again, and yet again. (Not uncommon when an actor gets stressed.) Finally, it was decided to reverse the camera angle, showing only the actor's back, so he could read his lines. All this took up valuable time.

After a few more shots and close-ups, it was time for my scene with Cliff. Quietly standing by in my Air Force uniform, I suddenly heard loud voices, and turned to see what the commotion was about. Cliff was raging at a woman from wardrobe. She had neglected to fit his uniform, which made him look as if he had a load in his pants. Adding insult to injury, the medals on his jacket were wrong. Off came the entire uniform. Forty-five minutes later, with Cliff's pants fitted and appropriate medals in place, we were ready to shoot. Now *I* was starting to become unglued.

My scene involved bringing coffee to Cliff and trying to make sense of his strange behavior caused by his oncoming mental breakdown. We rehearsed it, and the first take went okay. Then Cliff and Jud Taylor got into it about whether or not Cliff should sit or stand. Cliff wanted to sit, because he still wasn't satisfied with his fitted pants, and Jud wanted him to stand. The director won out.

Confrontations make me a nervous wreck, especially when I'm in the middle of one, and I was definitely in the middle of this one. Finally, the camera rolled again. I made my entrance into the office carrying Cliff's coffee. My nerves by now were so jangled that my hand holding the coffee cup was shaking, necessitating several takes. Cliff was also agitated and annoyed; no wonder our subsequent few takes were ineptly performed. The scene just didn't click. After what seemed an eternity, we got the shot the director wanted, and everyone moved on to the next scene. (When *Return to Earth* finally aired, I was mortified. It was the worst performance of my career. The film wasn't much to write home about, either.)

With filming over for the day, the actors, some crew members, and I were put on a van heading back to CBS in Studio City. Bottles of beer somehow materialized, and the party began. Five or ten miles along the way, the van pulled over for gas. Pulling in right behind us was Cliff's black limo. He immediately got out, walked to our vehicle, opened the door, and said loudly, "Sandra, why don't you grab your things and ride back with me."

I jumped up, collected my stuff, and happily followed Cliff to his car. I was seated next to him in the back seat when he turned to me and said, "Didn't want Dina's and my secretary trapped in a van with a bunch of rowdy drunks. Tough day, and things can get out of hand."

I laughed, and added that I was glad the day was over. As the limo weaved through traffic, we were soon talking like old friends. I teased him about having the limo this time instead of Dina. I reminded him of having previously met me at a Democratic fundraiser gala in Winston Salem, NC before I became a working actress. He remembered the gala, but not me. To my surprise, he shared a hilarious story about how he and Dina tried to conceive a baby, a tale that included him running down the streets of New York City to a sperm bank with a bottle of sperm in his pocket, and trying with Dina to time the precise intimate moments to conceive a child. Things eventually worked out, and their daughter, Heather, was born in 1978.

Before long, we arrived in Westwood. Cliff slid open the glass partition separating us from the driver. "Drop me off here," he said. "There's a film I want to see."

Turning to me, he asked, "Want to join me?" I shook my head and explained that I had a guy and a dog waiting for me.

We said quick goodbyes, and Cliff told the driver to take me back to CBS to pick up my car. "Take her to her car. Don't drop her off in the middle of the lot." As I watched him walk toward the theater, I realized that he was not only a great actor, but also a great guy.

That wasn't the last of my unexpected encounters with Cliff. A year or so later, I was invited by a soap opera writer to the Golden Globe Awards. We arrived a bit early, and were seated at a table toward the back of the room. Cliff arrived, and as luck would have it, passed right by our table.

I called out, "Cliff, hi! It's me, your secretary!"

He immediately turned, dropped to his knees, and exclaimed, "You're everywhere!"

Just then the spotlight hit him, and the emcee yelled, "There's Cliff Robertson!" With that, Cliff dove under our table. We were on national television, and this didn't look good.

I grabbed him by the back of his jacket and whispered, "Cliff, get up. This looks a bit obscene." He crawled out from under, stood up, winked at me, then proceeded to his table near the front of the stage. The show went on, and I didn't see him the rest of the night.

Our paths crossed once again a year or so later. Yeah. He was a SAG/AFTRA board member, and I was a member of a committee. We collided in the hallway of the SAG/AFTRA headquarters. This time, I got a hug. We chatted for a bit before going our separate ways. It was the last time we were to meet.

When I read that he had passed away in 2011, I actually cried, something I rarely do. It seemed in some way that we had bonded, not only because of our unusual repeated encounters, but also because we shared similar perspectives on Hollywood's follies and foibles. Cliff was an atypical A-lister. He was down to earth, considerate of others no matter their industry standing, and a man who always stood up for and lived according to his principles.

THE TONIGHT SHOW STARRING JOHNNY CARSON

1925–2005

"The Mighty Carson Art Players"

When it was on the air, every actor, be they bit player or star, dreamed of being on The Johnny Carson Show, as it was usually referred to. Suddenly there I was, a cast member of The Mighty Carson Art Players, a group of actors that performed irreverent skits with Johnny spoofing various aspects of popular culture. Sort of a snapshot of sorts to *Saturday Night Live* (1975–present), it was always an experience, for performers and viewers alike!

(Johnny Carson, the king of late-night television, was truly an all-American icon. He dominated his time slot for 30 years, from 1962 to 1992. Everyone over the age of thirty knows who he was, and slightly older folks enjoyed watching his good-natured skewing of politicians, celebrities, and commercials. The show always opened with his sidekick Ed McMahon proclaiming, "Heeeeeere's Johnny!" Several books have been written about him, his show, his moods, his lifestyle, and his five wives. (No, I wasn't one of them, not even close!) I won't reiterate what's already appeared in print. It suffices to say that Johnny won six Emmy Awards, memorably hosted the Academy Awards telecast from 1979 through 1984, and was honored at the Kennedy Center in Washington in 1993.)

Worrrrking with Johnny

When *The Tonight Show Starring Johnny Carson* (1962–1992) moved from New York to California in 1972, The Mighty Carson Art Players was recast with local Los Angeles actors. I was fortunate to get on the cast roster thanks to an often-intimidating NBC casting director, Sue Canter, who subsequently became a good friend. I don't recall how or why these two things happened, but they did. A Hollywood blessing.

It was a long time ago, and memory fades, but here are a few remembrances about the skits I appeared in with the one and only Johnny Carson. It was always a difficult show to do. One rehearsal and then tape it. That was Johnny's way. But there were compensations, beyond the credit and paycheck. The Burbank NBC studio where the show was based had a wonderful Green Room. This is a casual, comfortable room, liberally stocked with upscale food and drink, where actors and others involved in a show gather before taping. *The Tonight Show* had one of the best, and it was often the scene of some memorable moments that could never have seen the light of broadcast.

My first skit was set at a dance in a high school gym. Johnny played a nerd, and I played my usual charming self. The scenario had us start off happily dancing and making goo-goo eyes until the pneumatic Jayne Mansfield, one of the iconic sex symbols of the 1950s and 1960s, suddenly sashayed on camera. Johnny took one look at her, became hyper-aroused, flung me to the floor, and dashed over to her like a bee to honey. Not exactly Shakespeare, admittedly, but funny and risqué enough for the late-evening adults watching the show. Everything went fine from a technical standpoint during our one rehearsal earlier that day. But when

Johnny Carson, Peter Leeds, and Sandra de Bruin in
The Mighty Carson Art Players Columbo sketch.

we taped it for posterity, my leading man, perhaps inspired for
real by Jayne's ample charms, literally threw me halfway across
the set, where I landed in a very undignified, unflattering, and
painful heap. Fortunately, the camera remained on Johnny rather
than my flabbergasted expression. As I picked myself up, he and
Jayne continued their "nerd and sexy lady" hijinks. At least, I
thought to myself, I can now say I've been on *The Johnny Carson
Show*!

The next time I was on the show, Johnny and I did two
ad parodies. One was for Nike tennis shoes, the other was an
ensemble satire I don't recall. The Nike one was fun. Johnny,
again in manic amorous mode, chased me all over his office,
around his chair, and over his desk, much to the delight of the

studio audience and hopefully those watching at home on TV. Luckily, my Nike shoes won out, and I escaped his lecherous advances.

A month later, I was called back for yet another commercial send-up. This time, I was dressed in a bikini and tightly bound in rolls of transparent cling wrap, then placed delicately downstage, where I was to await with breathless expectation for Johnny to heroically unwrap me, only to get *himself* comically entangled in the wrapping. The dialogue was minimal, mostly ad libs, so it was a quick rehearsal. However, when we began taping, our star was a no-show. For several long moments I was alone onstage, feeling silly and exposed. Like I was waiting for Godot, if Godot were a late-night television host named Carson. Quickly improvising, I yelled out, "Johnny!" This brought laughter from the audience. (They always love being included in a joke.) It also brought the man, who rushed out and mindlessly entangled himself in our rather dubious premise. Afterwards, the director came up to me and said, "Good cover, Sandy." Johnny never said a word. Unfortunately, my scene-saving improv was edited out of the final aired version.

One of my favorite *Tonight Show* experiences was working with Bob Newhart. Now there is one marvelous man— talented, kind, and funny. Johnny opened the show with his usual topical monologue, followed by a one-on-one interview with Bob. It started with Bob's famous deadpan "Hello." It never changed, the epitome of a bad interview. Every time Johnny tried to get a conversation going with a question, Bob would answer with a single word: "Yes." "No." "Right." "Wrong." Finally, thoroughly frustrated, Johnny looked at his watch, took it off and pounded it on his desk. It was a hilarious moment, and the audience went wild. Later, I heard that many viewers didn't get it, actually thinking it was just a really bad interview. Johnny's audiences were usually pretty hip, but you can't reach everyone.

My skit during the same show came next with a take-off on homeowners' insurance. Johnny was the sleazy insurance sales-man, Bob and I the naive homeowners who had signed the con-tract. As the guys discussed the benefits of such insurance, the house fell down on top of me. To make a prolonged skit short, it ended with the insurance company refusing to pay for the house or for my injuries or death, calling it an "act of nature" not cov-ered by insurance. (Sound familiar?) All this transpired with great comedic style. However, I was mildly injured for real, and my favorite red dress was ripped and ruined. (The show always insisted that actors supply their own wardrobe if possible.) The production company never paid for my dress, even though ward-robe assured me they would. Johnny admonished the crew, but Bob was there for me in a heartbeat and genuinely concerned. I was touched.

My most memorable and well-known appearance was a spoof of the classic television series *Columbo*, starring Peter Falk. This skit is included on the *Best of Carson* DVDs and was analyzed in some detail in Christyne Berzesnyi's book *Columbo* (Intel-lect Ltd. New edition 2021). Johnny, of course, played Columbo, while Peter Leeds and I were an upscale corrupt couple plotting to leave town after committing grand theft and murder. The humor in this one skewed to the surreal, with Johnny as the dogged inspector unexpectedly popping up everywhere in our living room set—hanging from a hook in a closet, materializing inside a wall safe, popping up in a file cabinet, suspended upside down in a fireplace, emerging from a phonograph console—each appearance funnier than the last.

The sketch ran seven and a half minutes, and wasn't easy to perform on a single rehearsal. Johnny's cue card lines were in black, easy to read. Ours were red and blue, not so easy! Johnny was brilliant, mimicking Peter Falk's mannerisms: the methodical, rambling monotone, the studied air of innocent disorientation. I'd like to think that Peter Leeds and I held our own, shifting emotional gears through arrogance, deception, anxiety, guilt, desperation and, finally, resignation. It was an exceptional parody, flawlessly executed, and it almost made me a star. The capper was a surprise appearance at the end by Robert Blake, with Fred, the cockatoo from his hit show *Baretta* (1975–1978), perched atop his head. This brought the house down as Robert gave me a big hug. Definitely one of the iconic moments of late-night television, and a Mighty Carson Art Players favorite.

In the early 1980s *The Tonight Show with Johnny Carson* went from a 90-minute format to a one-hour show. The shorter run time, sadly, meant the end of The Mighty Carson Art Players. But it was a great gig while it lasted. Thank you, Johnny.

RET TURNER

1929–2016

Some stars become legends, but many legends have their own stars. Ret Turner was just that, a legend to the stars.

(Ret Turner was Bob Mackie's partner (think Cher's incredible out-fits through the years), and a costume designer in his own right. Bob created the designs, but Ret made them happen. He came to Hollywood from Marianna, Florida, where his parents were in the clothing business. He had ambitions to be an actor, but ended up as the head of wardrobe at NBC. Later, he was loaned out to CBS Television City, where most of the variety shows during the 1960s and 1970s were taped. Ret won five prime time Emmy awards for costuming such shows as The Dean Martin Show *(1965–1974),* The Carol Burnett Show *(1967–1978),* The Ann-Margret Show *(1968),* The Sonny & Cher Comedy Hour *(1971–1974),* Donny & Marie *(1976), and* Mama's Family *(1983–1984). He was also the consultant for the Academy Awards, SAG Awards, and the Emmys. The stars of these shows adored him and his personal attention to detail. There was nothing he couldn't fix or change on a moment's notice. Ret was the industry's "go to" person when it came to cos-tume design.)*

Take the Peas Out of My Top Ramen!

In the early 1970s, my true love, the writer William B. Murray (Bill), and I were looking for a house to rent. Without much ado, we soon found a lovely two-bedroom home just off of Doheny Drive in West Hollywood. It was perfect. That evening, we met at the property with the landlord, Ret Turner, a well-dressed, stylish fellow with a neatly trimmed red beard and hair to match. He wasn't very tall, but the elegant way he carried himself seemed to enhance his stature. Neither Bill nor I had any idea who Ret Turner was or what he did.

Having dispensed with polite introductions and brief social chit chat, Ret said, "The rent is $550 a month due on the first of each month. You can drop off your check at my house, which is just two houses down the street. You can move in now, but the rent will start next month. Does that work for you?"

"Well, yes. That's more than great," Bill replied. "But don't you want references or something?"

"No. You both look like responsible people, and I can't be bothered with unnecessary phone calls and paperwork. If you have any questions or problems, you have my number." With that, he handed us the keys to the house, jumped into his spiffy car, and drove off. I later learned that was *so* how Ret handled things.

During the time Bill and I lived there, we rarely saw or spoke with our landlord. Ret would wave at me when he saw me walking my dog, but that was it. Unfortunately, Bill and I broke up after a couple of years. He moved to Santa Monica beach and took with him all of his stuff and half of our furniture. I was emotionally devastated, and terrified of the financial responsibility he'd left me with. For days, I alternated between sobbing miserably and stewing in rage. Reality finally set in, and I knew I had to do something proactive. I left an emotional message on Ret's answering service. That evening, he appeared.

While I dramatically expounded on my situation, Ret walked around the house, noting the lack of furniture, including my bed.

"Where are you sleeping?" he asked.

"On the couch."

"Well, I think we can fix this. I'm in the process of evicting the couple next door. As soon as they move out, you can move there. The rent is $200 a month. Can you afford that?"

I was stunned. "Yes, of course. I can even pay $250."

"That's not necessary. Two hundred is fine. In the meantime, you can stay here until the place is available. Don't worry about the rent."

"I'll pay it back as soon as I can. I promise."

"It's okay," he said, and started to leave.

Then it hit me. This man didn't know anything about me. "You don't even know me," I said. "Why are you being so kind?"

"Oh, I know you," he said, eyes twinkling. "You are friends with Helen Funai and Howard Krieger, two of my favorite dancers on *The Dean Martin Show*. I've seen them here and you at CBS. The company you keep speaks volumes. In fact, I even wardrobed you for *The Carol Burnett Show*." (I was so nervous having been hired to do that show, and Ret was so low-keyed as he costumed me into a silly drummer outfit, that I didn't remember him.)

Flabbergasted by all this, I somehow managed to ask before he escaped out the door, "Who are you, and what do you do?"

"I'm Bob Mackie's partner. You do know who *he* is, don't you?" came his somewhat sarcastic reply. "We do costumes for Cher, Ann-Margret, Las Vegas spectaculars. I'm also under contract to NBC and currently loaned out to CBS, which is where we met. Now I have to go. Get some rest. Everything will be fine."

With that, he was gone before I could even mumble, "Thank you."

Several weeks later, the couple next door was forcibly removed by deputies from the West Los Angeles Sheriff's Department from what would be my home for the next eight years. In addition, Ret arranged for his personal assistant, Leslie Levitt, to oversee a complete renovation of the bungalow. Leslie was a wonderful woman who included me in all decisions—plush, dark-brown carpeting, newly painted walls, an updated bathroom with yellow-flowered wallpaper and matching shower curtain. It was nothing less than a mini-mansion. Leslie and I became fast friends, and she often invited me to dinner along with Ret. He and I would watch in awe as her two teenage sons devoured everything on the table.

Sadly, tragedy struck about a year later. Leslie was killed in the infamous 1980 MGM Grand fire in Las Vegas. When told to evacuate the hotel, she stepped into an elevator and never made it out. Ret was devastated and guilt-ridden. He had sent her to Vegas to work on some costume problems for their main show instead of going himself. That sense of guilt remained with him for the rest of his life. He unofficially adopted her two sons, who never lacked for anything from that day on.

Shortly thereafter, Ret's closest male friend, Joe, died of a sudden heart attack. He left behind a Lhasa Apso, which I quickly inherited, making for three dogs in my cozy castle. Thankfully, with Ret's permission, I found a wonderful home for the little pooch. My half-blind, aging manicurist was about to retire and in need of a furry companion. It was a three-way win: she got a pet, I got rid of another mouth to feed, and the dog got a forever home.

With two of his dearest friends gone, Ret found relief from his pain in long hours of work. As a result, he began to depend on me to take care of some of his personal responsibilities and properties. I became his de facto personal property manager, not only for his three rentals, but his own home as well. There was always something that needed doing—showing a vacant rental, buying a new appliance for this or that house, hiring tree trimmers, plumbers, exterminators—not to mention dealing with that one tenant who continuously locked herself out of her house. Ret offered to financially compensate me, but I wouldn't hear of it, so he made it up to me in other ways a thousand times over.

Not only did he take me to dinner almost every week, he professionally dressed me, plus the entire casts of several Los Angeles plays I was in, always free of charge. Playboy Bunny costumes for *The Habits of Rabbits* at La Mama Theatre. Period costumes for Shaw and Pirandello plays at the Melrose Theatre. The London scene from *California Suite* at the Zephyr Theatre. He even turned me into a Roman courtesan for a Sitmar Cruise newsletter in ten minutes with nothing but an old sheet and a pair of scissors.

My favorite Ret wardrobe story is when I auditioned for the hit sitcom *Three's Company* (1977–1984) during its debut season. The part called for an extremely well-endowed young sales clerk with the improbable name of Chloe Stoutmeyer, recently hired at the flower shop where co-lead actress Joyce De Witt's character worked. It was a big guest-starring role, with the episode built around the size of my chest, from getting the job to losing the job. My figure was good, but not as abundant as the part required. After reading the breakdown, I called Ret in a state of high anxiety.

Ret Turner with his Emmy Award, c. 1970s.

"What can I do that will make me look naturally voluptuous?" I wailed.

"Just wear a tight pair of jeans, a padded push-up bra, and a T-shirt," he said. "That's it." I did, and subsequently booked the job, much to the amazement of my agent, who was seriously dating me and was quite familiar with my anatomy.

Rehearsals at CBS went smoothly the first few days, with me just dressed in casual clothes as we did a table reading and scene run-throughs. Then I heard a rumble. I was on the verge of being replaced because the entire show and all of the main actors' reactions depended on my having Jayne Mansfield-like cleavage. John Ritter especially was having trouble. Apparently, when I auditioned, the producers and the director thought that my pushed-up, padded bosom was really me, and that wardrobe could enhance it to even greater proportions to fit the part.

I was somewhat of a wreck when I greeted Ret as he pulled into his driveway that night. Before I could open my mouth, he said, "I've heard. I'm the boob guy. I've got it covered." With that, he pulled from the passenger seat an enormous bra filled with birdseed. Yep, birdseed. It's natural-looking, and it moves, unlike padded bras. Ret's inspiration saved the day. I wore my birdseed bra through the rest of rehearsals and the taping.

The producers arranged for me to have a star's dressing room, complete with flowers and a telephone. Unfortunately, it required me to go up and down a spiral metal staircase. An enhanced bosom makes that impossible. I couldn't see my feet, and almost killed myself navigating the steps. The crew thought it was hilarious, but the producers panicked. My dressing room was subsequently moved backstage to a mundane ground-level room. Bummer! (I did get to keep the flowers.)

That episode of *Three's Company* was a tremendous hit, and was nominated for a comedy Emmy Award that year. To this day, I get fan mail for my poignant performance as the much put-upon Chloe Stoutmeyer. Unfortunately, there was a downside. My agent, Jim Gibson, had to turn down several job offers, because producers, directors, and casting directors actually thought all that birdseed was the real Sandra de Bruin. Jim felt strongly that I was on my way to becoming a star, and appearing as a sex symbol was not the way to go.

As far as my personal wardrobe, I'll never know if Ret thought it was his mission in life to make me more presentable, or if he just wanted to make me happy, as every couple of months an incredible outfit, coat, or pair of boots would be outside my front door, everything always a perfect fit. One rainy night, I was walking my dogs, wearing nothing but a plastic poncho, when Ret drove up. He rolled down his window, stared at me a moment, and yelled, "You're disgracing the neighborhood!" and drove off. The next evening, a beautiful red fitted Halston raincoat was hanging on my front door. (I kept that raincoat for more than 20 years.)

After the red raincoat gift, I determined that the least I could do was raise my own rent. Instead of the usual monthly $200, I wrote out a check for $225, attached a note explaining my decision, put the note and the check in an envelope, and slipped it under Ret's front door. The next morning the check and a note were under my front door. The note read, "Can't accept this. It will put me in another tax bracket. Love, Ret."

Ret's mother, Mrs. Turner (she insisted on always being called Mrs. Turner), an eccentric southern woman, and his nine-year-old niece, Jean, visited Ret in Los Angeles every summer for two weeks. While Ret was at work, Jean would spend most days with me doing the usual tourist stuff: the beach, the studios, Disneyland. Or we'd just hang out together while I pursued my acting career and took care of Ret's properties. She was a delightful child. Her grandmother, on the other hand, was a character with a heart of gold. She would call me any hour of the day or night to pick up the "nasties" (translation, dog poop) in front of Ret's house. She kept her Southern Comfort at my house, since Ret objected to her drinking, and would arrive regularly for her evening pick-me-up. Oftentimes, she would come to my house in tears, having just had a battle with Ret's equally eccentric maid, Goldie, over some silly thing like a flower arrangement, and demand that I fire her. It was always something amusing but outrageous with Mrs. Turner.

Eventually, Ret did fire Goldie. But he paid her for years *not* to clean his house. Again, so like Ret.

Other than hosting his mother and Jean every year, Ret rarely entertained, except for his annual Christmas Day party. That was the party of the year. Celebrities, friends, and nobodies were invited. Cher showed up one year, as did our gardener. Anyone who had nowhere to go was included. Ret spared no expense. There was catered food from top restaurants, an open wine bar, and Valley Gal parking attendants. Even when he eventually cut back and it became more casual, it was a celebration to look forward to. Singing, dancing, good food. What could be better? In the 40 odd years I knew Ret, I missed only one Christmas party, and only because I was out of town.

As they always seem to do, all good things come to an end. In the mid-1980s, I fell in love and married a fun and energetic man with two children. With great trepidation, I moved into their home in the Larchmont Village area. Ret rented my bungalow to his adopted son, thereby keeping it in the family. A few years later, my marriage disintegrated. After the divorce, I stayed on in the house for a while, but on the spur of the moment moved to Denver, Colorado. My acting career had slowed down, and I thought I could be a big fish in Denver's little pond.

That was the first and only Christmas I did not attend Ret's holiday gathering, but I did call him. He and I and the whole gang were on the phone for at least an hour. Afterward, I cried for hours. I missed him so much.

It took about eight months to realize that there was no real professional film acting pond in Denver, so I returned to Los Angeles. I called Ret, hoping that one of his properties would be vacant. No way! But he did recommend that I look in the

San Fernando Valley, where I subsequently found an adorable Spanish-style house in Studio City.

A week or so later, after arranging the furniture and getting my dogs settled, Ret and I had a long catch-up dinner. Things for him had taken a downward turn in the ten years I was more or less out of his life, despite his having received twenty-three Emmy nominations and five wins. America's taste in television had changed. Variety shows were replaced by serial dramas. Bob Mackie's empire collapsed, including his recently opened New York shop, which went into bankruptcy. This seriously affected Ret's finances, as they were partners. On top of all that, Ret's contract with NBC was not renewed. He was now working as an independent contractor for the Academy Awards shows, the Emmys, and Las Vegas spectaculars.

Picking up the pieces, Bob and Ret rented a large warehouse just off of Ventura Boulevard in Studio City. They each had their own enterprise in the shared building, but often assisted each other. Bob continued designing for the stars, and Ret opened his own costume-rental business.

The warehouse was just a mile from where I lived, so Ret and I were soon having what we called our bi-monthly tryst. He had his favorite places, where he was known and treated like a king. He insisted on always paying, often saying, "Learn how to be a lady and just smile and say thank you." Occasionally, I would get to our designated restaurant early and hand the waiter my credit card, with strict instructions that lunch was on me. Our luncheons, along with Ret's Christmas parties, went on for years.

Ret had many attributes, but unfortunately, running a business was not one of them, and the costume rental business slowly declined. His employees were congenial, but mostly inept.

I learned later that they often took advantage of him; shopping for unnecessary things, hiring their friends, taking time off, etc. He consciously or unconsciously ignored what was happening. Later, after briefly working there, I tried to alert him, but he would hear none of it.

Before long, Ret's health became a serious issue. His back gave him constant pain, although it turned out to be a hip problem. In 2014, he was diagnosed with prostate cancer. At first, it seemed to be under control, but soon he was confined to his home, attended by round-the-clock nurses. Seeing as his business needed help, I volunteered to work part-time and sort and display the massive amount of costume jewelry that was piled up all over. After a few weeks, Ret's assistant, who was now in charge, insisted I should be paid at least minimum wage, which Ret felt strongly I should accept. This went on for several months.

Throughout the last six or seven months of Ret's life when he was confined to his home, I would take him lunch once a week. The routine was always the same. I would call ahead and ask what he wanted to eat. He would say either Top Ramen or tuna fish. It never varied. Ret would sit in his favorite living room chair while I put together lunch in the kitchen, and we would banter back and forth like an old married couple, much to the amusement of his nurse. "Don't forget the salt!" "Salt isn't good for you." "My plants are dying." "I'll water them later; I'm cooking." "You don't know how to cook." "I know that, don't rub it in." And my favorite, "Take the peas out of my Top Ramen!"

In the early months of 2016, I made my way to Ret's house with his usual lunch request for Top Ramen, ordered the night before. When I arrived, there were emergency vehicles parked in front. I made my way through the paramedics to Ret's bedroom.

He was moaning in agony, with tubes in his arms and an oxygen mask covering his face. When he saw me, he pulled off his oxygen mask and whispered, "Oh, I'm so sorry, I forgot to call you to cancel lunch." Those were the last words Ret ever spoke to me. He died a few days later.

His funeral was at Forest Lawn in Burbank. It was a closed event, and only a few of us, about twenty people, including Cher, were in attendance. A month later, his niece, Jean from Georgia, arranged an impressive "Celebration of Ret's Life" at the Wilshire Boulevard Temple. Hundreds of folks were there: celebrities, friends, relatives, and blue-collar workers. Although pricy wine and champagne flowed and stunning flower arrangements decorated the room, Jean had arranged for Ret's favorite (un-chic) food to be served: tuna fish, cheese fish crackers, overcooked sushi, and, of course, Top Ramen. Ret would have been so pleased.

Ret Turner is truly a legend. I'm not sure Hollywood deserved him. I know I didn't.

MARIE WINDSOR

1919–2000

There is nothing like a dame, nothing in this world.
This lady was the epitome of a dame—strong, beautiful,
and fun, with no pretenses.

(Marie Windsor, a former Miss Utah standing 5'9", began her acting career in theater in 1940, played numerous bit parts in films throughout the early and mid-1940s. She landed more substantial roles near the end of that decade, notably in the iconic film noir Force of Evil *(1948), and eventually moved on to starring roles in many B pictures. She became one of the leading film noir archetypes, the femme fatale who gets her man into bed and into trouble. Audiences loved to hate her as she earned the title "Queen of the Bs." Among her most notable films (and her personal favorites) are* Hellfire *(1949),* The Narrow Margin *(1952), and* The Killing *(1956). The latter, though not financially successful, later became a cult favorite. Despite the type of characters she played in these films, Marie was quite the opposite in real life. She often said, "I liked the parts, but wouldn't have liked them in real life." Marie's second marriage (the first was annulled) was to Jack Hupp, a Beverly Hills realtor. Together, they raised a son and a stepson. She was a member of the Church of Jesus Christ of Latter-day Saints, an active member of the SAG board of directors for twenty-five years, and the founder of the popular SAG-AFTRA Film Society. Later in life, she guest-starred in numerous hit television shows. She also*

returned to the stage, acting in many Los Angeles stage productions. She received a well-deserved star on Hollywood's Walk of Fame in 1983.)

My Muse, Marie Windsor

I first met Marie Windsor at her home in Beverly Hills in the mid-1980s. She was hosting an informal get together for Actors Working for an Actors Guild (AWAG), a group of working actors started up by Charlton (Chuck) Heston. Being that Chuck, our fearless leader, had recently appointed me AWAG's secretary, I was invited to the meeting. The group was trying to keep the Screen Actors Guild (SAG) exclusive to film actors. Extras, dancers, theatre actors, television hosts, commentators, recording artists, newsmen, etc., all had their own unions, but wanted to become a part of SAG, which offered more benefits and more power. SAG was intent on including all of these performing artists under its umbrella in the face of what had become a two-party political struggle. Since AWAG was comprised of high-profile celebrities as well as lesser-known working actors like me, we were being labeled "elitists."

Arriving at her home just off Coldwater Canyon and parking in her spacious driveway, I noticed an array of lights going on and off and gates opening and closing automatically. Later, I learned that all this electronic wizardry was Marie's son Ricky's passion and pastime. I wandered into the house and made my way to the living room, which was filled with about twenty people sipping wine and nibbling on chips and dips. After a short rah-rah meeting, the room turned into a get-together cocktail party. Feeling somewhat out of place, wine glass in hand, I ambled around the living room and bar area, studying the paintings on the walls.

From behind me came a distinctive gravelly voice. "Well, I'm glad *somebody* is paying attention to my paintings." I turned to face Marie Windsor, a lovely, tall lady with liquid brown eyes, long dark hair pulled back, and neatly trimmed trademark bangs accenting her eyes.

"Oh, I didn't know you were a painter," I responded.

"It's a hobby, that's all. What do you think of them?"

"Some of them I like; others I'll have to study before commenting."

Marie chuckled. "Ah, a straight talker. I like that. No wonder Chuck made you secretary. Get yourself another glass of wine and circulate. Egos abound, but we're all quite nice and fighting for the same cause."

Taking her advice, I made the social rounds, found a sofa, and was shuffling my meeting notes when Chuck approached with a bottle of Chardonnay and insisted on refilling my glass. Marie joined us, and the three of us sat chatting about acting and AWAG. It was obvious that Chuck and Marie were close friends. I was delighted to be in their company. Soon, however, I was out the door and headed home, but not before Chuck Heston walked me to my car. Yep, little old me.

Marie phoned early the next morning. Dispensing with social chit-chat, she said, "I noticed the boots you were wearing last night. I like them. I need a pair. Would you come shopping with me this afternoon? We'll go to the Beverly Center."

Recovering from my surprise at her call, I replied, "Thank you. And, yes, I'd be delighted to go shopping with you."

"Fine. You mentioned you live in West Hollywood, which is on the way, so give me your address and I'll pick you up at 11:00."

She promptly hung up after I gave her directions. I quickly realized that Marie wasn't one to waste words.

Marie arrived on the dot in her vintage light-blue Cadillac. (I learned later that she and her husband, Jack, drove matching Caddies.) What a ride that was. Marie drove like a maniac through the winding back roads of Beverly Hills, but we somehow arrived unharmed at the Beverly Center, and began the serious job of shopping for boots. Marie proved easy to please, and quickly decided on the boots she wanted, two pairs. Bypassing (to my surprise) the ritzy, elegant restaurants at the mall, Marie preferred that we have a quick lunch at the food court. She treated. We did a bit more shopping, then headed back to my house. Marie accepted a glass of wine, petted my dogs, and offered multiple suggestions for improving the decor. Too drab for her taste, she said it needed color. Thus began our personal friendship, along with our professional work for AWAG.

Marie was intent on keeping SAG a guild for working actors *only*. She was relentless, constantly writing letters and memos soliciting new A-list AWAG members. Computers were not part of everyone's life in the 1980s, so each letter had to be individually written. It wasn't long before Marie had me up at her home on a daily basis, creating a filing system for her and furiously typing personal letters to the rich and famous to get them to join the cause. Yet each day without fail, she would stop everything in the afternoon to phone her mother back east. They would talk anywhere from fifteen minutes to a half-hour. Every mother should have such a loving daughter.

Working together did pose one major problem: neither one of us could spell. Marie once summoned her Spanish-speaking maid and asked her how to spell "exclusivity." The poor woman, dish towel in hand, stood there as if her feet were nailed to the floor. Eventually, the spelling problem was remedied, or at least mitigated, after I bought each of us the book *20,000 Words Spelled and Divided for Quick Reference*. (Still available, believe it or not.)

Simultaneously, I was working with Chuck, organizing and taking notes of AWAG meetings, rallies, and press conferences, while also endeavoring to keep an acting career going. Fortunately, these icons lived only a few miles apart, enabling me to dart back and forth with ease. Nada, my dog, often accompanied me to Marie's house, where she and Izzy, Marie's dog, would hang out together, as Marie and I toiled away on behalf of our cause.

Marie and I became quite close while all of this went down. Jack and Ricky welcomed me like one of the family. (Ricky once went out of his way to help me pick up a scattered stack of papers I had inadvertently left sitting on top of my car.) In the evenings, we would sit together and enjoy the cocktail hour. I rarely stayed for dinner, however, as Marie's cooking was upstaged only by her lack of spelling acumen. In retrospect, Marie and I were a perfect team. Neither one of us could spell or cook, we found the same things funny, we loved our dogs, and, most importantly, we shared the same set of values. Hit hard, but don't hit below the belt.

Regretfully, after about six months, AWAG folded. SAG was relentless in positioning AWAG members as "elitists," and the SAG members bought it. A SAG vote was taken, and the extras, now called "atmosphere," became SAG members. Within several years, all entertainers working in every genre became part of what is now called SAG-AFTRA. It went from a guild to a union, and currently numbers approximately 160,000 members. The friendly, warm, and helpful atmosphere was now a cold, corporate business marked by constant infighting.

My friend and muse, Marie Windsor,
in publicity photo for *The Killing* (1956).

Happily, Marie and I continued our friendship following AWAG's dissolution, albeit not on a regular basis. We would shop or have lunch or dinner every week or so. Often, I felt her new cause was me. On two occasions, she fixed me up with well-heeled guys. They were fun, but nothing to take seriously. Marie was also concerned about my acting career. In 1987, she starred in *The Bar Off Melrose* at the Melrose Theatre in Hollywood. Although she was the lead, it was really an ensemble play, with numerous characters milling about the eponymous bar. Marie called me, her voice elated. "It's about an aging actress watching her old movies at a bar on Melrose. That's me!" Then she asked, "Didn't you tell me that you were a member of the Melrose Theatre?"

"Yeah, but that was about ten years ago. I'm not anymore," I replied, feeling bad vibrations from the past.

"Doesn't matter. Come audition for a part. I'll put a good word in for you. You'll be in like Flynn."

"Oh, Marie, that's so sweet of you, but I can't. I really can't."

"What do you mean, you can't?" she answered, taken aback.

"I left the Melrose Theatre under ugly, painful circumstances, and I don't want to reopen that door." (Looking back, my decision was the right one, as I went on to bigger and better personal and professional things.)

"Are you going to tell me about it?"

"Nope. It's the past, and the past is where it should stay."

"Well, okay. Will you at least come to the play?"

"Of course! I wouldn't miss seeing you perform for anything."

I did, and she was brilliant. In fact, that year she won the Los Angeles Drama Critics Circle Award for best actress, an honor well-deserved.

We kept in touch over the next few years and did our usual things: lunch, shopping, and cocktails. In the late 1990s, her health began to decline, and the arthritis in her back accelerated, perhaps owing to her tall stature. She was in constant pain, but, being stubborn, would not change her longtime doctor (who was out of step with modern medicine), much less get another medical consultation. Adding to the problem, in my view, was her adherence to the Church of Jesus Christ of Latter-Day Saints. I believed they were religious shysters interested more in remuneration than redemption.

Strong pain pills were rationed by her doctor and/or the Latter-day Saints, for whatever reason. Marie was soon walking with a cane, then a walker. Jack, meanwhile, was also failing. Before long, they were both confined to hospital beds, side-by-side, in their bedroom. Sad as it was, it was also in a sense somehow lovely and romantic.

I could relate numerous stories about the last year in Marie's life, but two of them stand out for me.

Snapshot 1: I arrived at her house one day expecting our usual conversation about my life, her career, her health. Without preamble, however, she informed me that her black Labrador needed his daily diabetes shot. Summoning her live-in maid to bring in the syringe, Marie told me to go outside and give this poor, elderly dog his shot. There was Izzy, happily snoozing in the garden. I approached him lovingly, and was about to stick this pointed needle into his shoulder, when he suddenly looked up and into my eyes. I panicked. There was something about stabbing this sweet creature with a needle. I just couldn't do it. I went inside and confessed to Marie.

"Oh, for God's sake, Sandy," she responded sharply. She called the dog to her bedside. "Now, lift him up and give me the syringe." Before I could blink, it was done. Marie threw the syringe in the trash and lay back down in bed. I let the dog outside and returned, only to be greeted with, "You've got to toughen up, Sandy. To get ahead in this town and in life, you've gotta be strong. The good life is not made for the weak. Now, go and get us a glass of wine."

Marie continued her barrage as we drank, but with less of an edge. It went something like this: "You have it all. Don't be afraid to use it, and don't be afraid of hurting someone. They'll survive, and they'll get over it."

I thought about her words as I crawled into bed that night. It dawned on me that they applied to her, and that's what made her Marie Windsor, the lady I loved and admired. I realized that I had to get tougher if I was to be successful.

Snapshot 2: Despite her physical issues, Marie loved to be out and about. We spent one of our last days together having lunch at one of her favorite places, the Beverly Glen Deli, a celebrity hang-out in a mini-mall just south of Mulholland Drive, where the rich and famous go to relax and not be bothered by tourists. When I arrived to pick her up, Marie, loaded with painkillers, zipped down the hallway on her walker with tennis ball glides attached to the wheels. Hubby Jack, seated in his wheelchair in the foyer, was delighted to see Marie happy and energetic enough to get out of the house for a while.

Just as we were about to exit the front door, the comedy gods intervened. Marie stumbled, and her walker, with all of her weight pressing down on it, ran over Jack's foot. Jack yelped with pain, the dog barked in sympathy, and a nurse rushed in to lend assistance. What did Marie and I do? We broke into hysterical laughter. Insensitive? Sure, but we couldn't help ourselves. It was a scene right out of a screwball comedy. A half-dead woman run-ning over her half-dead husband's foot with a walker? You can't write that kind of stuff. It would never get past the three-piece suits in their ivory towers.

Luckily for us, the nurse quickly determined that Jack would be fine. Jack, thankfully, took the incident in good humor, despite his obvious pain, and insisted that we stick with our luncheon date. What a great guy.

Marie was in high spirits as we ate, happy to be out and about for a change. Afterward, we browsed the high-end shops and the pet store before returning home, only to be told that Jack's foot had been broken and that he was at the UCLA Medical Center Emergency Room. Marie broke down, but was assured that Jack's foot was in a cast and that he would soon be home. I helped put her to bed, watched some television with her, and went home. It was one of the last occasions I spent quality time with her. To this day, I'm glad and grateful for that fun, silly excursion. I think Marie felt that way too.

Marie passed away on December 10, 2000. Her memorial service was held on January 6, 2001 at the Louis B. Mayer Theater in Woodland Hills, designed for residents of the Motion Picture & Television Fund. A huge crowd turned out to honor her. On the entry wall were between 50–100 professional and personal photos of this unforgettable icon. Chuck Heston gave the main memorial speech. Unfortunately, Jack was too ill to attend.

Oh, Marie, you taught me so much. I loved you so much, and I miss you so much. May I someday be as important to someone as you were to me.

ROBERT WISE

1914–2005

**What does one say when introduced to director/producer
Robert Wise, an American film icon? All I could say was,
"Thank you, Mr. Wise. It was nice meeting you."
That changed as the years rolled by, and a meaningful
friendship developed.**

*(Robert Wise was a man of all genres, directing forty-two films in
his fifty-year career. They included war films, musicals, film noirs,
westerns, science-fiction movies, historical and action-adventure
epics. He began his career as an editor in 1939. His outstanding
work in that capacity on* Citizen Kane *(1941) for Orson Welles
eventually put him in the director's chair. His first film as director,* The Curse of the Cat People *(1944), was a huge hit, and led
to numerous award-winning successes. J.R. Jordan's book* Robert
Wise: The Motion Pictures, *examines in detail all of his films.
Among the most memorable were* The Set-Up *(1949),* The Day the
Earth Stood Still *(1951),* Somebody Up There Likes Me *(1956),*
I Want to Live *(1958),* Odds Against Tomorrow *(1959),* West
Side Story *(1961), Academy Award winner* The Sound of Music
(1965), Academy Award winner The Sand Pebbles *(1966),* The
Andromeda Strain *(1971), and* Star Trek: The Motion Picture
*(1979). A four-time Academy Award winner for directing and pro-
ducing, Wise was also president of the Director's Guild for several
terms, and president of the Motion Picture and Television Acad-*

emy for two years. His mastery of nearly every film genre remains unequalled.)

Robert Wise, but to Me Just "Bob"

I had only been in Hollywood about a year, and had done just a few television shows, when my agent, Arnold Soloway, an A+ guy with a B+ Agency, got me an audition for the small part of a frightened lab technician in the film *The Andromeda Strain* (1971), directed by Robert Wise at Universal Studios. Six actresses, myself included, were brought to the Universal sound stage, the biggest one on the lot, to audition. We all lined up in front of Bob. After walking up and down the lineup a few times, he paused to look at me, and, gesturing as if to shoo away a dog, seemed to dismiss me. I started to leave, then turned back, and said, "Thank you, Mr. Wise. It was nice meeting you."

"Where are you going?" he replied.

By way of explanation, I imitated the gesture he'd just made. "Oh, well, I meant. . . ." and he did the gesture in reverse, beckoning me to where he was now seated. He turned to his assistant director and said, "You can let the rest of the girls go." That's how I came to be cast in what would become a cult sci-fi classic.

A script was dropped off at my front door the next day. My role was easy to memorize, consisting of just a few lines and two scenes. During one scene, my character runs away from Kate Reid, playing a scientist who has just collapsed in front of a laboratory door. I yell out, "She's got the germ! She's got the germ!" My other scene occurs near the end of the film, after James Olson's character has climbed a metal ladder up an underground silo to deactivate a self-destruct mechanism on Level 3 of the substation. He pleads with me to help him find the deactivation unit, but I back away in the opposite direction.

A few days later, I was on a huge Universal sound stage about to work with the director of so many amazing films. Call it serendipity. As a teenager, I lived in New York City a few blocks from where the street dance numbers in *West Side Story* were filmed. Several times, I walked over to the closed set and watched from afar. Yeah, it seemed I had come full circle.

On my first day of filming, one of the extras didn't show up, and due to matching issues, the scene could not be filmed. Mr. Wise said, "Come back tomorrow." I returned the next day, but I was a nervous wreck. Three times I said my two lines, and then started running, as my character was supposed to. Each time, Mr. Wise would say, "Come back and do it again." His blue eyes twinkling, he said, "Okay, this time I want you to say your lines, and then keep running until I say *cut*. I want to hear your footsteps fade out."

I did my lines, and then ran, and ran, and ran. I ran all the way around that enormous stage and back to Mr. Wise. The entire crew cheered. Mr. Wise smiled. "Okay. We got rid of that nervous energy. Now, let's do it again." We did it again, and it was fine, just the way he envisioned it.

Several days later, I returned to film my scene with James Olson, who was a lovely man. There was minimal dialogue. James spoke several lines to me as I silently and fearfully backed away from him after he had made his dangerous climb up the silo. Although I didn't have any lines, I played my part convincingly. Mr. Wise expressed his satisfaction. I came away with the feeling that I was beginning to accomplish something in my career. I headed home, merrily singing, "There's no business like show business!" That night, I sat down and wrote Mr. Wise a colorful thank you note.

A month or so later, I received a personal invitation to the film's premiere at Grauman's Chinese Theater in Hollywood. I was thrilled, and spent several days deciding what to wear. Mr. Wise personally greeted me at the entrance and guided me toward the bar. The premiere was a benefit for the Los Angeles Inner City Cultural Center. Serendipity again. My good friend, C. Bernard Jackson (whose story appears elsewhere in this book), who years earlier played the bongo drums for my dance class at UCLA, was now the artistic director of the ICCC, which he had co-founded in 1965. It was incredible running into him and seeing how far he had come.

Mr. Wise and I remained in touch over the next few years. Whenever I had an audition, or was working at a studio where he had an office on the lot, I would stop by to say hello. If he wasn't there, I would always leave a note. His secretary of many years always greeted me with a big smile. On one occasion, I had a late-evening audition with a producer doing an independent film at Universal. I first stopped by Mr. Wise's office, and told him there was no specific part mentioned, only that the producer just wanted to meet me. My *Andromeda Strain* director didn't say anything, just nodded. After some chit-chat, I dashed across the street, to be greeted by the well-dressed but sleazy producer, who immediately insisted that I have a glass of wine. A half hour or so went by while he paid me compliments, plied me with more wine, and promised to "make me a star." This was not my vision for success. My personal proximity warning system was in the red, and I was starting to panic.

With impeccable timing, there came a sharp knock on the door. Reuben Cannon, Universal Studios' Head of Casting, was

Film director Robert Wise on the set of *The Andromeda Strain* (1971).

Emoting dramatically in my film debut, *The Andromeda Strain* (1971).

standing there. Reuben said he was checking on me, and that all actors and actresses not actually working had to be off the lot before he could go home. I jumped up and rushed out the door with him. Out of the corner of my eye, I spotted Mr. Wise, standing in front of his office, hands in pockets, observing the scene. He waved and called out, "Goodnight."

I knew that checking up on actors in this way wasn't the norm, so I asked Rueben why he had done so. He replied, "Mr. Wise called my office and said he was concerned about you. He thought someone should check on you, as it was getting late." I later found out that Robert Wise (who soon became Bob to me) harbored an aversion to producers and superstars taking sexual advantage of starlets and studs. He was disgusted with Tinseltown's reputation, which unfortunately persists to some degree today.

Five years after *The Andromeda Strain* was released, Bob's wife of thirty-three years, a lovely actress named Patricia Doyle, passed away from cancer. He was devastated by the loss, as the marriage had been a strong and happy one. In 1976, Bob was at MGM prepping for his next film, *Audrey Rose* (1977). I stopped by his office one day to visit, and we talked about this and that. My stomach was rumbling, so I asked if I could buy him a hot dog. He cracked up, and said, "Don't think my stomach can handle a hot dog. I have a better idea. How about we go to the commissary?" We did, without further ado. I had a delicious chicken salad and ate all the bread.

I didn't think anything of it until Bob called a few days later and asked me to dinner. That night, unexpectedly, something clicked, and we began what turned out to be a six-month romance. It was an exciting and wonderful time. I spent almost every weekend at his home on Broad Beach Road just north of Malibu. It was a setting straight out of a movie. Anybody who was anybody lived on Broad Beach. Bob had a three-story modern house right on the beach, complete with buzzers, perfect lighting, even a dumbwaiter going from the ground level to Bob's bedroom on the third floor. I often brought along my shaggy dog, Nada, who also formed an attachment to Bob. One time, I put her in the dumbwaiter, but she wasn't used to such an unusual mode of transportation, and arrived at the third floor in a catatonic state.

Much to Bob's credit, he made it quite clear shortly after we became an item that he didn't believe in nepotism or favoritism, and that would apply to me. (He wouldn't even hire his own son as part of his crew.) That was more than okay with me. I was happy to avoid that kind of awkward scenario. However, Bob was happy to recommend me for a role in other directors' films should the occasion arise, which is how I landed a part in the 1978 film *Gray Lady Down*, which starred my friend Charlton Heston.

On Friday nights, Bob would often host special screenings at his home. A wide variety of folks were invited: Julie Andrews, Russ Tamblyn, Bob's family, several of my friends, and both of our dogs. Bob would show whatever film was popular at the time. Afterward, the guests feasted on a lavish buffet. He had a lovely French couple that lived in during the week. They cooked and served, and everything was always flawless. After dinner was cleaned up and the guests had gone, Bob would pour us a last glass of wine, and we would sit outside or inside, depending on the weather, and discuss the film while listening to the waves crashing on the shore and watching the moon dancing in the background. It was magic.

Making my life perfect was the fact that Bob's family, celebrity friends, and his help were extremely receptive to me. They knew I made Bob happy, and that's what they cared about. Occasionally, however, embarrassing situations occurred. One Saturday evening, Bob had run off to get something for dinner. I was alone in the kitchen, chopping up a salad with a rather fearsome-looking knife, when the front doorbell rang. I managed to use the intercom to ask who was there. A vaguely familiar English voice said, "It's me, Julie. I have your pot. Open up and I'll leave it inside the gate."

The front entrance was at street level, three stories up. I frantically tried to figure out how to electronically open the gate, but to no avail. Finally, in frustration, I ran up the stairs to the front gate, forgetting that I was still clutching the knife. There behind the gate stood Julie Andrews, and there I stood on the other side, disheveled, out of breath, with a knife in my hand, undoubtedly looking like an escapee from the loony bin.

I'll never forget the look on Julie Andrews' face. And she'll probably never forget the look on mine. Before she could scream for help, I suddenly realized how deranged and dangerous I appeared. Dropping the knife, I tried to put something like a normal person expression on my face, and breathlessly babbled, "It's okay! I'm a guest! I don't know how to work all the electronic buttons, and couldn't open the gate. I'm just making a salad. Bob went to get some fresh tomatoes. He'll be right back."

Julie sized me up for a moment, seemingly unsure whether to let down her guard. After reassuring her that I posed no threat, she relaxed, and I relaxed. We exchanged a few niceties, she handed me the pot, and went on her way.

When Bob listened to my embarrassing story, he called Julie to confirm that all was well. That is, after he stopped laughing. He spent an hour the next day showing me how to work all of the electronic features in his modern smart house. At one of Bob's subsequent screenings, Julie mischievously asked, "Still greeting guests with a knife, Sandra?"

Bob wasn't much of a social guy, with the exception of those Friday night screenings. He loved walking on the beach with his beloved Irish setter, and enjoyed going out to dinner, sometimes with other people, but that was about it. He also loved opening nights at the theater. We went to the invitation-only opening night of *A Chorus Line* in Los Angeles in 1976. I remember panicking about what to wear, before settling on a full-length, dark-brown sheath, a simple gold chain, gold hoop earrings, and gold strap sandals. Bob favored simplicity, and he glowed when he saw me, which gave me a ton of confidence when we made our entrance.

One weekend, we went to San Francisco. It was such a special trip. We stayed at the Fairmont in a luxury suite, walked and shopped on the wharf, had dinners at the best of restaurants. Most importantly, it was just the two of us. By now, he knew what wine I drank, and I knew what made him happy. We were comfortable together. It was the best of life.

Soon after, it was Academy Awards time. Naturally, Bob received a special invitation, not only because of who he was, but because two years earlier he had produced the Awards show. For some reason, however, he didn't mention it to me. I finally brought it up. He just looked at me without saying a word for what seemed like an eternity. Finally, he came out with, "I don't want to go. They are long and tedious, and my back and knees can't do it. But if you really want to go, I'll arrange for you to get an invitation." I was stunned. How could anyone not want to go to the Academy Awards show, especially if they were offered celebrity seating?

"I don't want to go without you," I instantly responded. "Where's the fun in that?"

"Think about it. You've never been, and I know it's every actress's dream," he quietly replied.

I hesitated. I looked at this wonderful man, obviously very uncomfortable with his decision. All I could say was, "Maybe we can go another year."

"Maybe we can, but this year we can still make it special. How about we stay home, order lobster and champagne, and enjoy the sunset." We did just that, and a lovely evening it was. Unfortunately, our romance didn't last for another year, and I never got to go to the Academy Awards. It's the one thing in our relationship I regret to this day.

Each weekday through most of our time together, Bob worked on his film *Audrey Rose* (which starred Anthony Hopkins and Marsha Mason), prepping, shooting, and editing. I would often join him for lunch and hang out on set watching him set up the shots and handle the actors. Anthony Hopkins often ignored the markers (but then, he's Anthony Hopkins), so Bob would compromise, while Marsha Mason needed constant reassurance. Susan Swift, who played their 11-year-old daughter, was a joy. Once in a while, Bob would stay over at my bungalow rather than drive back to Broad Beach. On those occasions, we would always go out to dinner, as early in our relationship he surmised that cooking was not my forte. Once I made him a crock pot dinner. He did the polite thing and raved about it, but when I offered to buy him a crock pot, he emphatically declined.

Towards the end of our romance, Bob went to New York on business, and while there invited my parents to dinner before presenting them with orchestras seats to *A Chorus Line*. They were thrilled. My Dad told me later it was a bit strange to meet a guy who was only about ten years younger than him who was in love with his daughter and who made it clear that he intended to marry her.

Yeah, Bob was old school and believed in marriage, not just having a companion and lover. Bob wanted an old-fashioned, stay-at-home wife. I was in my mid-thirties, and thoroughly enjoying having a career in acting that was actually paying the bills. I never envisioned being a star, but I loved the process of acting, the people involved, and the fun of the chase. I didn't want to give it up to just become a wealthy housewife to a film icon.

This eventually became an issue, and we started to spend more time apart. Before long, his wife-to-be entered the scene. After a month or so, it came to a head, and we broke off our relationship. Soon after, he married his second wife, Millicent Franklin, and they moved to a deluxe condo in Century City. Bob loved his beach home and his Irish setter, and it must have been very difficult for him to leave it all behind. His dog died, the French couple moved to Oregon, and his loyal secretary was let go. About that time, due to Millicent's insecurity, Bob ended our friendship. I heard talk that she was not popular among his friends and family. Ironically, a year or so later I saw her at Saks Fifth Avenue, and found out why. She was making a scene at the counter where scarves were sold. All I heard was an indignant voice. "I'm Mrs. Robert Wise!" Oh, how he would have hated that display.

The last time I saw Bob was on a street in Beverly Hills. He looked older, sadder, and worn-down. We chatted briefly before he went on his way. He remembered to ask about my parents, which I thought was especially nice, and typically Bob.

Inexplicably, the Academy of Motion Picture Arts and Sciences paid no special tribute to Robert Wise at the Oscar Awards following his death in 2005. The acknowledgment was very brief. His picture, along with other film luminaries who passed away that year, was onscreen for less than two seconds. This was unacceptable to me. From the 1940s through the 1970s he was one of the most important directors in Hollywood, having won multiple Oscars along with the many other industry achievements listed above. He was an enormous presence in Hollywood, respected by all, and a lovely man. I still think of him so fondly and so often. Maybe it's time to watch for the tenth time *West Side Story*.

SANDRA de BRUIN

1940–

Me, Myself and I—A Hollywood Adventure

Being an actress in Hollywood is like living your life on a roller-coaster. It's up and down, fast and slow. One day you're a winner, the next day you're a loser. The trick, of course, is not letting those losing days defeat you, seeing things in prospective, maintaining a sense of humor, and above all being true to yourself and your values. I have tried to do all of these. I can now look back and say with a smile, "I was a working successful actress." And, I did it my way. During the 1970s and through the late 1990s, I had guest-starring appearances on dozens of the most popular television shows, did commercials, industrial films, and print, live modeling, and multiple game show appearances.

Given my rather ubiquitous CV, it's more than possible that my face and/or name flashed into your consciousness, if only for a few hopefully pleasurable moments. Theater kept the creative juices flowing, and I once got a sensational review in the *Los Angeles Times* that only my mother could have written.

Yeah, I arrived in Hollywood well trained and street smart, and with an unshakable set of values that stood me in good stead through the good times and the lean times. The vignettes in this chapter detail a few of my follies and foibles along the Hollywood road I traveled. They are stories of audition fiascos, commercial disasters, airport encounters, and, yes, moments of fame.

AUDITIONS

Furballs in the Vents

There is a phrase that all actors are familiar with, although they may not always be happy to hear it: "going straight to producers." This means that when one is up for a role, there is no preliminary audition with the casting director. Oftentimes, such an audition beforehand can be of great benefit, as the casting director can impart valuable advice about what the producer and director are looking for. Some actors, however, resent it, and consider it condescending and beneath them. Not me! I loved a preliminary audition, not only for any tips I could glean, but for helping me get the lay of the land. With all the competition out there, I always took every advantage I could get.

I well remember one "straight to producers" audition at Paramount back in the mid-1980s. The character was a sergeant aboard a spaceship. The actual audition was just a couple of pages, although the role itself was larger. As I rehearsed at home, it sounded like a fun project: a comedy aboard an interplanetary vessel. The scene took place in the captain's quarters and concerned what I assumed to be a comical problem within the ship.

Come the big day, I dressed how I thought a female space sergeant would—no-nonsense white shirt, dark skirt, hair swept conservatively back—and headed confidently to the studio.

When I arrived at the waiting room, a secretary was checking off names of the other actresses up for the part as they came and went. Soon enough, it was my turn, and into the producer's office I marched.

Five unsmiling people sat behind a long table in a claustro-phobic-inducing, windowless room: two producers, the writer, the director, and Megan, the casting director, whom I had previously met for another project. She was an Irish lass, Black Irish, that is: dark-brown hair, light-blue eyes, and a Gaelic sense of humor. A replica of me! A good sign, I thought to myself.

The casting director always reads with the actor, so after making brief introductions, Megan said, "Ready? I'll lead you in."

Playing the Captain, Megan began, "Sergeant, we have a major problem on ship. An emergency."

"An emergency, sir?" I responded in character.

"Yes. Apparently, there is a cat aboard, and there are furballs in the vents."

I paused, taking this in, then repeated with a fine sense of comedic timing and a wide-eyed, dumbfounded expression, "Furballs in the *vents*?" It's called reaction comedy. Mary Tyler Moore, one of my acting heroes, was a master of this on *The Dick Van Dyke Show* (1961–1966) and her own sitcom, *The Mary Tyler Moore Show* (1970–1977).

Megan and one other person in the room let out stifled giggles, so I assumed I had hit on just the right tone. Then one of the producers emphatically cut in. "No, no, no! This is very serious. Furballs in a spaceship vent can cause the ship to explode, not to mention killing everyone aboard. Do you get it?"

"A cat aboard a spaceship causing furballs in the vents! Sorry, I thought it was a . . . a joke," I stammered.

With that, the writer jumped up, and with an appropriate amount of pomposity, declared, "I've researched spaceships, and if such a thing was to occur, it would be catastrophic!" Ah, the writer's ego!

Megan quickly and thankfully interceded. "Sandra, this is a drama. Comedy is double-spaced and drama is single-spaced. You do know that, don't you?"

"Yes, of course, but obviously I didn't notice. So sorry," I humbly replied.

"Why don't you step outside and work on it from a dramatic angle, and then we'll have you read again."

"Thank you. I'll make the adjustment," I responded gratefully as I rushed through the door to the outer office where the other actresses were waiting to read.

I informed the secretary that I had been asked to wait and read again. Being asked to stay and read again usually means that you are being considered for the part, which of course makes other actors uneasy. I could sense them all giving me "wonder what she has" or "what she did" looks. I was tempted to tell them how I had given the scene a comedic twist, but that would have been mean. Besides, I was quite sure, due to the barely concealed fury of the powers that be, that I was out of the running, so why shouldn't one of my competitors get the part?

Unfortunately, doing an instantaneous about-face on an audition one has worked on in a certain way is easier said than done. Try as hard as I could, I could *not* get the comedy out of that line. In my mind, I substituted furballs in the vents with deadly snakes, which would, of course, be terrifying and not at all funny. That didn't work. Next, I visualized a ferocious pussycat grooming herself and happily retching furballs in the spaceship vents. No go!

Several actresses took their shots in the inner office while I struggled to refocus. Finally, I was called in to read again. There I was, confronted by those same faces looking very serious and intent. They acted as though they were casting *Gone with the Wind* (1939).

To make a short story even shorter, I gave them my best dramatic performance, acting *horrified* that there should be such *dastardly* things as furballs in the vents. After Megan and I finished reading the scene, I said the usual thank you and rushed out the door, past the secretary, out of the building, and into the sanctuary of my car.

That evening, I wrote a note to Megan thanking her for the audition and apologizing for my comedy debacle. I signed it, "Furballs in the Vent?" She responded several months later by having me audition for another project, which I thankfully booked.

The spaceship film never premiered or aired as a television movie or series.

Mrs. Pratt

It was almost two o'clock on a Friday when my theatrical agent, Arnie Soloway, phoned. He had just received a call from John Conwell, a casting director at CBS. I had worked for him before on a soap opera and knew him casually socially. He was casting a television movie of the week about teenage angst. John wanted me to come no later than four o'clock and read for the small feature role of Mrs. Pratt, the mother of a teenage daughter. It was the early 1990s, and the sides couldn't be sent to me because I didn't have a FAX machine, so Arnie suggested I go in early to look them over.

Since John had specifically requested me, with no special instructions, I assumed he just wanted the stereotyped housewife, so I dressed more or less in my everyday attire: jeans, tennis shoes, shell top with a denim shirt over it, and hair in a casual ponytail. It was a young, refreshing mother look, not the least bit character-looking. Wrong! The name, Mrs. Pratt, should have given me a clue.

Upon arriving at CBS, the secretary gave me two pages of sides. On the first page was the character description and the scene breakdown. It read as follows:

"Mrs. Pratt's daughter, Maxine, is having a barbeque for her friends in the backyard, when Robbie (the lead teenager in the show) knocks on the front door. It is opened by Mrs. Pratt, a woman in her mid/late 30s: ample, nervous, and haunted-looking."

Her few lines were upbeat. "You must be Robbie! So glad to meet you. Come in."

Further down the page in the next scene, Mrs. Pratt is talking and serving hamburgers and drinks to the teenage guests. That was it. At no point in either scene did Mrs. Pratt's behavior fit the above character. I was perplexed, so I asked the secretary if there was another scene or perhaps a story breakdown that I could look at to get some insight into Mrs. Pratt. Why was she nervous and haunted-looking, much less ample? (I'm 5'7" and weigh 120 pounds dripping wet.)

The secretary graciously looked through other sides on her desk and said, "There's nothing here, and I haven't read the script, so I can't help you."

Shortly thereafter, I was called into John's office and introduced to the young director and the middle-aged bald writer responsible for all these vivid adjectives. Jumping in before John had a chance to start the reading, I repeated the description "ample, nervous, and haunted-looking. Why?"

Everyone looked blankly at each other, so I inquired further. "I haven't seen the script. Is there something in it that explains this

Portrait of a working actress.

description? Is there a family crisis? Is the daughter pregnant? Did somebody die? Or does Mrs. Pratt have a lover in the closet?"

Nothing. No one could explain why this woman was ample, nervous, and haunted-looking. Finally, the writer feebly mumbled that the woman was nervous about having a teenage party.

I paused, obviously not pleased with his answer. "Oh, okay."

Realizing that his response was less than satisfactory, he leaned forward and said, with a presumed air of great knowledge and authority, "*But,* you don't have to be all three at once!"

Dumbfounded and stifling a laugh, I looked over at John. It was too much for him, and he burst out laughing, as did the director. A moment later the director said, with a huge smile, "Whoa, don't know if I can direct that with just three lines."

Let's give credit where credit is due. The writer paused only a moment, then joined in the laughter, all the while muttering something about being more judicious with his use of adjectives.

I finally read my few lines and left. The part went to an ample actress who at least looked somewhat nervous and haunted.

The Denver Fiasco

In the summer of 1995, I decided to temporarily move to Denver, as my career didn't seem to be advancing in Los Angeles. I had heard good things about filming in that area, and was hoping to be a big fish in a little pond. Alas, there was no pond! Upon arriving, I signed with the best agent in Denver. Judy (I won't give her last name) was impressed with my resume and appearance. During my short stay in Denver, however, she arranged only one good audition. It was for a Los Angeles film company shooting on location there, but I didn't get it. Other than that audition there was always a catch: payment under the table, no official SAG contract, auditions in offices with no lighting or backdrop, etc.

One March afternoon Judy called to say I had an audition for a small part in a Stephen King film based on one of his short stories. It took place in a macabre hotel about 30 miles outside of Denver, and auditions were being held there. In Denver, with its March snow and icy roads, such a drive is lengthy and quite unnerving.

She continued enthusiastically, "They requested you, so it looks really good. If you're hired, you'll spend the night there and film the next day."

I started to ask about a contract, screen credit, working conditions, and whether or not I'd get at least two day's pay, but then passed, as it was a Stephen King film and definitely an opportunity.

I drove down to her office, picked up the sides from her receptionist, and returned home. Settling down with a glass of wine, I excitedly read the few pages given to me. The description read as follows: "A nude cadaver sitting in a bathtub singing a ditty." The dialogue then followed with some incoherent disgusting song. Nothing else.

I immediately called my agent, thinking and hoping that there had been a mistake. Nope. That was the role. Through clenched teeth, I said, "Well, I don't do nude work, much less nude cadavers, so send my regrets."

"What?" she retorted.

"You heard me," I fired back.

She paused a moment. "This isn't working out very well for us, is it?"

"No, it isn't," I replied. "Perhaps it's better if we void my contract with your agency and I move on."

"Done!" she replied, and hung up.

That did it for Denver. The next day, I made arrangements to return to Los Angeles. A month later, I was back in the Golden State, never to leave again. As far as I know, that film never left the editing room.

COMMERCIALS

Falstaff Beer

In the mid-1970s, before my career really got going, my piggy bank was running on empty. Yeah, I was working part-time as a secretary, so the rent was paid, but that's about all that was paid. My small television roles to date were nothing to write home about, and certainly not lucrative. An actress/model friend suggested I get a commercial agent, because that's where the money was. She arranged for me to meet with her agent, Mary Webb Davis, who headed the agency of the same name. This was a high-end modeling agency that had just opened a television commercial department, where my friend thought I would fit in.

I bounced excitedly into the office on La Cienega and was immediately ushered into Mary Webb Davis' spaciously impressive office. Behind an imposing desk crowded with 8x10 pictures of famous models sat a no-nonsense, fashionably dressed woman in her mid-forties. She gave me the once-over as we benignly chatted about one thing and another. Then out of nowhere came, "You're definitely not the model type."

"Well, I. . . ."

She cut me off before I could say another word. "You're not tall enough, you're not thin enough, and I doubt if you can pass the pencil test."

"The pencil test?" I repeated, not having the vaguest idea what she meant.

"Yes, the pencil test. Something all my models must pass. You put a pencil under each breast, and if the pencil falls down, you pass. If it stays in place, you fail. You have a very nice figure, but a bit too round for a model, and not round enough for *Sports Illustrated*."

I stood there, a bit nonplussed, not sure if this was a compliment or an insult. Before I could respond, Ms. Davis said, "However, you're personable and quite pretty, so you might work out in our commercial division." With that, she hit a phone buzzer and instantly arranged for me to meet Beverly, her commercial agent.

Beverly turned out to be warm and friendly. After perusing my pictures, my resume, and me, she said she would see how I fitted in with the other young actresses she represented and get back to me in a few days.

I went home, somewhat deflated, but with crossed fingers. Maybe, just maybe, this would work out. That evening, another friend rang up to tell me about a cattle call audition the next day for Falstaff Beer. All actors who showed up had to have a Screen Actor's Guild (SAG) card and an agent. I had the card, but no agent, or did I? My friend didn't have to twist my arm very hard to convince me to try out for the commercial, even if I wasn't quite kosher agent-wise.

Armed with the necessary info—character descriptions, time, and place—I set off for the appointed place the next day, head shot and resume in hand. What a zoo. I counted at least a hundred anxious actors hoping to be chosen to extol the virtues of the beer named for the Shakespearean character Sir John Falstaff. I signed in, checked off "SAG card," and gave Beverly at Mary Webb Davis as my agent. Above the sign-in sheet was a notice that read: "There will be no call-backs." Which translates as: nail it now, as there won't be a second chance. The actual audition, though, didn't exactly present a Shakespearean challenge, just a group of beautiful young people laughing and dancing the night away while enjoying that great Falstaff flavor. The typical beer commercial of that era. I did my thing and went home.

My phone rang late afternoon the next day. Could it be? Yep, it was Beverly. Not bothering to conceal her excitement, she blurted, "I understand you're my client and you just booked a Falstaff commercial." Cue shrieks and yells on both ends of the phone. When we regained our composure, Beverly said, "Come by tomorrow, and let's sign a contract." Commercial agents are always thrilled when a client books a national commercial, just like theatrical agents when a client books a film or a recurring role on a TV series. It's money in their pocket. Suddenly, that client is gold.

The commercial shoot went fine and took only a day. It aired on and off the tube for a while, but never made the agency or me rich. What it *did* do was make me a favorite of Mary Webb Davis, which began sending me out on auditions for print jobs and industrials. Most of them eluded me, but I finally nailed a big print job: a five-day shoot for AT&T produced and directed by Saul Bass, the iconic graphic designer and filmmaker who created title sequences for such films as *Vertigo* (1958), *Psycho (1960)*, *West Side Story* (1961), *The Shining* (1980), and *Goodfellas* (1990). We shot all over Los Angeles: the airport, the beach, Beverly Hills, studio lots, and even the *Los Angeles Times* building downtown. I supplied most of the constantly changing wardrobe, but the production company did have a wardrobe van standing by loaded with clothing and jewelry available for any and every ensemble. Mr. Bass personally approved of every outfit I wore for the shoot. It was fun, but exhausting.

After the shoot was over, Mary Webb Davis promptly sent Mr. Bass a bill for my services. It ran to $500 per day, totaling $2,500. Models are paid *after* the client pays the agency, which then pays the talent, usually a week or so after the job is finished. In the modeling profession the agent is totally responsible for collecting whatever is due. There is no union like SAG to challenge or help them recover payment. As it turned out, Mary tried unsuccessfully for weeks to get paid. She phoned, she sent weekly invoices, she even had her lawyer send a threatening letter. No response, and no money.

Finally, I went to her office and got a copy of the invoice, which now included my personal dry-cleaning expenses and late fees. After grabbing a sandwich and coffee, I went straight to Saul Bass' Hollywood office, a small, one-story building off Sunset Boulevard with a front patio. The receptionist was not happy to hear the reason for my visit, and immediately ordered me out of the building. I complied and went and sat in the outdoor patio.

Soon thereafter, I was told to get completely off the property, so I moved over to the adjoining wall of the neighboring business. There I sat for hours, nibbling on my sandwich and loudly telling anyone and everyone who went into Mr. Bass' office not to work for him because he didn't pay his employees. Some folks paid no heed, but others did. Word eventually got back to Mr. Bass about the unwelcoming lady at the front of his building. After about five hours, the receptionist stomped out, threw a check at me, and snapped, "Mr. Bass said to tell you that you'll never work for him again."

"Good!" I replied. "Do thank Mr. Bass for the check." With that hard-won check in hand, I joyfully returned to the agency office. Mary looked at the check, smiled, and exclaimed, "Well, he paid the late fee, but not your dry cleaning. Are you okay with that?"

"Perfect!"

"Are you sure? We can try a rebilling for the balance."

"No, no, no. Let's just cash the check and be done with it."

"Okay," she replied, calling to an assistant and handing her the check. "Get this to the bank before he stops payment on it." He didn't, and two days later I was one rich gal.

Several years later, I was booked for a small part on one of the many films about Marilyn Monroe, and somehow it involved

Saul Bass, probably as the graphic designer. He obviously didn't remember me when we were shooting on the set. The same scenario played out, though, as Mr. Saul Bass once again refused to pay his talent. This time, however, the film was under SAG jurisdiction, and they finally nailed him. It took months for a check to arrive, but it did, including an extraordinary late fee.

After the Saul Bass check adventure, the Mary Webb Davis agency sent me out on everything, most of which I didn't book. At Christmas, I was given the agency's leather-bound Daily Reminder, a gift presented only to top clients. I was so pleased.

A few months later, Mary called me into her office and said, "SAG has asked me to send a representative to serve on its Commercial Contract Negotiations Committee. I would like to send you. Are you interested?" I jumped at the chance. Thus began my involvement with SAG politics. (That saga will not be told in this book.)

As time went by, Beverly decided to open her own commercial agency, and I went with her. I stayed with Mary for print jobs, but those eventually dried up. As she had said during our initial meeting, I just wasn't the "model type." However, my time with Mary Webb Davis will always place high among my favorite Hollywood memories.

Luigi's Pizza

My commercial agent called me rather late one evening: delighted, surprised, and quite obviously excited. "You just booked a pizza commercial!" she shouted.

"What?" I replied, equally taken aback. "There must be a mistake. I haven't auditioned for any pizza commercial."

"You mean I didn't get the gig?"

"I got the gig! Didn't get the car."

"I know that, but the casting director from NBC just called. She said she knew you from *The Johnny Carson Show*, and you're perfect, and there was no need for you to audition. It's for Luigi's Pizza, and it's a national."

This was exciting. A national commercial implies that it will air across the United States, not just locally. That means big residuals for actors and agents alike, *if* it runs. The "if" is always a given, as quite often a commercial is filmed, but never airs or is put on hold for months, tying the actor up by preventing them from doing similar product ads.

"This is great! I love pizza!" I screamed. It was the early 1970s, and pizza was the edible craze of the moment.

My agent told me the shoot was in two days, congratulated me, said she would call back soon with details, bid me goodnight, and rang off. I hollered and jumped up and down like a mad thing. My dog helped me celebrate, barking furiously and running around in circles.

Not a moment later the top costume designer Ret Turner, my landlord/neighbor/dear friend, called. "I gather you have just heard that you got the Luigi's Pizza commercial," he said in his usual wry delivery.

"Yes! How did you know?"

"I'm doing the wardrobe." Ret was head of the wardrobe department at NBC and Bob Mackie's partner. Think *Cher*. (See chapter on Ret Turner) "You'll be the sexiest pizza server in town."

"No, no, no, Ret, I don't do sexy. Sexy is a dime a dozen here in town. I don't want to be one of them."

"Actors!" he countered. "Calm down. I know that's not you. How about adorable and sexy?"

"Yeah, that works."

With that, he said, "Turn the dog off and go to bed. I'll see you at NBC."

Two days later, there I was on NBC's Luigi's Pizza soundstage. To no one's surprise, it reeked of pizza. Lots of pizzas. Pizzas in a quantity like I've never seen before, and hope to never see again. All of these pizzas were to be served cold to the actors seated at various tables on the restaurant set, as steam coming off hot pizzas would pose a problem for the cameras.

Even more mind-boggling was the presence of five chimpanzees, each with a musical instrument, standing by waiting to perform as the Luigi's restaurant band. In those days, Screen Actors Guild (SAG) rules and safety measures weren't strictly enforced, so most of the chimps weren't chained, just holding onto their handlers' hands. They were cute, lovable, and friendly, all decked out in festively colored diapers. Cast and crew alike were enchanted and constantly petted and cooed over them. Being the animal lover I am, I instantly fell in love with them all, especially the drummer. We connected. He so loved his job!

Ret's idea of "adorable and sexy" was to dress me in Italy's national colors: a skimpy green, white, and red skirt; white V-neck blouse with the same colors on the sleeves; white boots; and a ridiculous-looking white waitress hat. I looked like a human version of the Italian flag.

For the first scene, the cameraman panned across the tables filled with happy hungry customers munching Luigi's delicious pizza. The simian band, on a slightly raised stage, was literally going ape: blowing horns, shredding guitars, pounding drums. Of course, the instruments were muted, but what did they care? These musical primates were having the time of their lives.

Cut to scene two: Enter me, Sandra, the sexy yet adorable Italian flag girl, carrying a pizza just like real servers—one hand under the tray, pizza held precisely even with my head—adorably and sexily making my way to a designated table. So far, so good, right? Well. . . .

As I passed by the band, the chimp doing his best Ringo Starr impersonation, the one I had instantly bonded with, suddenly leaped off his stool, and with a huge grin smacked me on the fanny with his drumstick. I went flying, the pizza went flying, and instant mayhem ensued. The cast and crew burst into uncontrollable, unstoppable laughter. Encouraged by the humans, the other chimps joined in the fun. Deserting the bandstand, hooting and grunting and shrieking and laughing, they ran riot around the set, jumping on actors, hugging them, and snatching pizzas off tables, all while avoiding the best efforts of their handlers to contain them. It was total chaos.

Now, this was an AFTRA shoot, which means that it was shot on tape, not film. As such, the director usually spends most of his or her time in a booth watching the tape and yelling directions to the actors through a microphone. It's very impersonal. One feels like a character on a chessboard.

This particular director, caught up in the bedlam he was witnessing, totally lost his cool, and began shouting hysterically over the microphone, "Actors and crew: *stop* laughing! Do not engage the chimps. You're encouraging them. Stop it this minute!" His admonitions caused even more havoc.

The more he yelled, the more everyone—including and especially the chimps—misbehaved. It took over a half-hour before order was restored and calm once again prevailed on the set. Well, sort of.

The NBC maintenance crew arrived and cleaned up the mess. The handlers got their chimpanzees somewhat under control, but had to put chains around their feet and/or necks, much to the dismay of the actors and crew, as we had become so fond of our cuddly, impish forebears.

We shot the scene several more times, but it never really worked. In fact, the commercial never aired.

That evening, Ret phoned and said in his usual dry delivery, "I knew you had one of the best asses in Hollywood, but who would have thought it would cause such chaos?"

"Is that a compliment or an insult?"

"Take it as a compliment. You've earned it. How about Chinese tonight?"

"Anything but pizza!"

Picnic Candy Bars

It was the early 1970s, and my life as an actress had just begun. After two years of dedication, hard work, and the occasional flash of brilliance, I was finally counted among the elite members of the Melrose Theatre. Although that venerable facility was known primarily for acting workshops and shows, outside directors and producers sometimes called on its actors for projects. Such was the case one midsummer when a television production group from England began shooting Picnic Candy Bar commercials throughout the United States. It was a non-union outfit, which upon arrival in Los Angeles not only required non-union actors, but actors who could ride horseback western-style. Western movies were a tad passé in the 1970s, but still popular in Europe, where the commercials would be aired. It was a buyout for $200, meaning the actors would receive just that as a lump sum payment.

Having been born and raised on a Tucson, Arizona ranch, I had learned to ride before I could walk. (An accomplishment that my Dad took great pride in.) To this day, I ride like the wind. Of course, I was immediately chosen to be in the commercial, along with six other actors, some of whom *claimed* they could ride, but obviously couldn't. We were to shoot in Saugus on a large ranch with wide-open spaces. The actors would mount up and then race across the range, dismount, and happily gather around a campfire and eat Picnic Candy Bars. Simple.

Came the day of the shoot, we gathered at the designated location arrayed in our personal finest western garb. Not something most actors have in their closet. One gal had on fashion ankle boots, another wore a gold chain belt instead of a leather one, and one guy sported freshly pressed designer jeans. My attire was just what I wore when I rode on the weekends: worn-out Levi's, a red plaid shirt, and expensive classic western boots. Waiting for us was the English producer/director, a film crew, a medic, various wranglers, and six saddled horses. The horses were magnificent, beautifully groomed and full of energy. They were showbiz studio horses and hadn't been ridden in over a month, as most shows were on summer hiatus. They were ready and anxious to run. Studio horses are specially trained and know film language, often better than actors. They know and react to such words as standby, rolling, action, and cut. Believe it or not, after hearing "cut" or passing red flags, they automatically stop and return to the starting point and do the same thing over and over. Amazing.

As introductions went around and horses were being assigned, one girl panicked and refused to go near her mount. Another fel-

My one "Sophia Loren" picture.

low fell short of being brave, but agreed to try to ride. He too was nixed. That left just five of us to do all the riding.

I was assigned Buddy, a beautiful sorrel horse with a white blaze down his face. He was a lead horse, which means he's out front and the others follow. The macho head wrangler stood by as I mounted. He adjusted the stirrups, all the time calling me Little Lady.

"He's a good horse. Just hold him back or he'll leave the other horses in hell," he advised. With that, he gave Buddy a friendly pat on his neck and stepped back.

We all were mounted and at the starting point. The director raised a bullhorn and yelled, "Standby." All the horses suddenly came alive, arching their necks with ears forward.

Next, he yelled, "Action!" Buddy reared up and almost unseated me, then took off like a bat out of hell. Within seconds he was *way* out front, leading the pack to the half-mile finish line.

A few seconds later, I heard a rider's voice behind me shout, "Straight ahead to Los Angeles, Sandy!" In less than a minute I crossed the finish line, which was marked with red flags. I tried reining Buddy in, but he didn't respond. Nor did he see the flags, or didn't care. He just kept going.

Our English director, in his plummy British accent, shouted through his bullhorn, "Young lady, bring that horse back here! This is not a fox hunt! We have a commercial to shoot!" Buddy kept going, and as skilled a rider as I was, I couldn't stop him. I started to panic. Finally, I realized that Buddy had gotten his bit above his front teeth, which meant he might as well not have had a bit at all. Holding the reins tight, I leaned forward as far as I could, grabbed the left rein as close to the bit as possible, and spun him to the left. He fought for a moment, then stopped. But I saw the glint in his eye that said, "Almost got ya!"

After Buddy and I collected ourselves, we galloped back to the starting point, where we were greeted less-than-enthusiastically. After dismounting, I led Buddy up to the head wrangler who had helped me mount. Through gritted teeth, I snapped, "Tighten the bit and check the cinch before I ride him again."

"You're gonna ride him again?" he asked smugly.

"You bet. Buddy and I now have an understanding," I countered.

He smirked, but then his sunbaked face lit up and he said, "Sorry about that." He knew exactly what had happened. "You ride well. Stick around and I'll get you a job in a real movie."

After everyone had settled down, we proceeded to do the same scene numerous times. Those incredible horses would race to the flags, stop, and then casually lope back to the starting point and do it again.

After several successful takes, we moved on to the scene in which the riders gather around a campfire to eat Picnic Candy Bars. Our "acting" consisted of laughing and drinking water out of tin cups. This scene also necessitated multiple takes until our director proclaimed himself satisfied. How many candy bars can one eat? Yeah, you got it. We all went home sick as dogs, vowing never again to so much as *look* at another candy bar.

Several days later, most of us were once again hired by the same English company to do a dune buggy commercial on Malibu Beach. This time, I was definitely not the star. My prowess with horses sadly did not transfer to motorized vehicles. First, I lost control of my dune buggy, and it ended upside down, with me likewise. Then, my dune buggy got stuck in the ocean. Lastly, I got bitten by a jellyfish, at which point I was quietly retired to the sidelines. Not a successful venture, but at least I got another $200.

Fast forward a year or so. My true love, Bill Murray (the writer, not the actor), and I were in Rome, where he was on assignment for *Playboy*. We decided to take in Sam Peckinpah's new film, *Bring Me the Head of Alfredo Garcia* (1974). Bill was a good friend of Sam's, and I had also met the famously controversial director on several occasions. Sam was not one of my favorite celebrities, but nevertheless off we went to see his film. They were already showing commercials in England before the main attraction. The movie houses in Rome also followed this custom.

Bill and I sat eating our popcorn as the lights dimmed, expecting to suffer through some boring ads before the feature presentation. Then a strangely familiar face suddenly appeared on the huge movie screen. It was me, in glorious Technicolor! There I was, riding Buddy, hell bent for leather, hair flying in the wind, riding like I had a date with destiny—or a campfire gathering to enjoy some delicious candy bars after a hard day on the trail. Picnic Candy Bars, of course. Yep, I upstaged Sam Peckinpah's film, no doubt about it.

VIGNETTES

The Tonight Show with Jay Leno
1992–2014

Occasionally, an actor gets a gig that starts out bad, gets worse, and ends disastrously. Bottom line: "Show me the money!"

It was a weeknight, and I was scheduled to spend the evening at a casting workshop called Reel Pros. Unfortunately, that afternoon my dog, Patches, had impaled himself on a small wire fence. Frantic, I rushed him to our vet in Hollywood. Although it was just ten miles from my home in the Valley, Los Angeles traffic made it seem at least double that. I didn't get back until almost seven, then had to arrange for a friend to doggie-sit while I was gone. Having gotten everything and everyone under control, I gulped down a glass of wine, grabbed my head shot and resume, and raced to the workshop just after eight.

The NBC casting director was a nice young fellow from what is usually referred to as *The Jay Leno Show*. He brought scenes (called "sides" in the acting world) from various shows and assigned them to all the actors present. Mine was a three-person comedy scene. Everyone rehearsed outside for about fifteen minutes, then returned to the room. Soon, it was our turn to perform onstage. It went well. Everyone laughed, and the CD smiled. I went home, hugged my dog, and went to sleep, knowing I had aced it.

The next morning, my agent called and excitedly told me I had booked the *Jay Leno Show*. It was to be a takeoff skit of *The First Wives Club*, a 1996 comedy with a star-studded cast about three divorced women who seek revenge on the husbands who dumped them for younger women. I would be working with Lucy Lawless, aka Xena the Warrior Princess, and Ivana Trump. Yep, that Ivana, the first wife of Donald Trump, our soon-to-be president. This was awesome.

Even though cue cards would be provided during the taping, I received a script in advance to memorize. My being cast was doubtless due to my comedic performance at the workshop, plus the fact that I had been a semi-regular member of The Mighty Carson Art Players on *The Tonight Show Starring Johnny Carson*. (See earlier chapter.) The powers that be felt confident that I would be able to cut it, even though I was not a recognizable star or celebrity.

A few hours later, the owner of Reel Pros called, bursting with indignation, admonishing me for being a few minutes late to the workshop and having alcohol on my breath. She ranted for a minute or two about workshop standards, conduct, rules, etc. When I could get a word in edgewise, I gleefully informed her that I had just booked *The Jay Leno Show*. Dead silence. I then assured this prohibitionist that I never drank alcohol before a workshop, the previous night's exception due entirely to the day's accumulated stress over my beloved dog. The conversation finally ended with a forced, "Congratulations."

Two days later, still buzzed about the gig, I arrived at NBC around noon, parked my car, and checked in with the guard at the back gate. As I started walking through the parking lot toward the sound stage where *The Jay Leno Show* taped, I encountered a scene of mass confusion. This unexpected and unwelcome sequence starred a film crew, executives, an ambulance, multiple firemen, and a horse. Everyone, with the exception of the poor, bewildered horse, was shouting, giving orders, and running around like fools. As a disaster film, it might have been entertaining. As a portent of what this might mean for my skit, not so much.

It turned out that the director of the show had decided to give Xena the Warrior Princess a special introduction. The idea was for her to gallop, sword grasped firmly in hand, up to the sound stage on a mighty steed. You know what they say about best-laid plans. The horse—no doubt accustomed to more congenial terrain—unfortunately stumbled, and the Warrior Princess found herself suddenly de-saddled and flying through the air, landing, not softly on some medieval sylvan lawn, but on the hard NBC parking lot pavement. Thank the gods that the sword was made of plastic, or she might have fatally impaled herself. However, the poor woman was seriously injured and eventually taken to the hospital. The horse was returned to his stable in disgrace.

Somewhat dazed by the surreal spectacle I was witnessing, I made my way to the show's office, only to find everyone there in a state of hysteria. I was told to relax and grab a cup of coffee while another actress was found to replace Lucy Lawless. Several hours went by, which I spent chatting with the grips and catching up on the show's gossip. Seems that no one liked the executive female producer, the massive curtains from which Jay opened the show were far too overstated, and trouble was brewing within the band. Jay wandered around aimlessly, as confused as everyone else. That's as close as I got to Jay Leno. Neither he nor any one in charge bothered to keep me informed about what was happening.

Then, like a bad third act, more madness set in. The producer had booked a replacement for Xena, only to discover that Ivana Trump had suddenly decided not to do the show because it required *acting*, not just schmoozing with Jay. Ivana doesn't act, she only schmoozes and shops!

After seven interminable hours, I was told that I could go home. The skit was canceled. I sighed, signed out, jumped in my car, and headed for the leftover bottle of chilled wine awaiting me at home. As you've probably guessed, it tasted damn good. When the bottle was empty, I called my agent to relate the sad saga. After he got done cracking up, he said, "Well, you can put it on your resume. You were officially hired. You showed up and were ready to work. At least you'll get paid."

Not quite. A week or so went by, and no check. My agent finally called the show, only to be told, "The skit was canceled. We're not going to pay her for doing nothing." The fight was on!

After a few more weeks passed, I insisted that my agent demand that I not only get my contractual salary—a mere $450—but also a late-payment fee. The show's unlikeable producer went berserk. (Six months later, Jay Leno thankfully fired her.) My agent suggested we back down regarding the late fee, saying that I'd never work on *The Jay Leno Show* again. But I held my ground and insisted he go for the late fee. A month later, the check arrived. Yeah, late fee included.

The sort-of good news: All my friends thoroughly enjoyed the story of my almost-gig on *The Jay Leno Show*. Only in Tinseltown can one arrive on time for a job, know their lines, then never get to tape the show because Xena the Warrior Princess fell off her horse and Ivana Trump opted to go shopping.

Raiders at the Airport

**Sport fans encompass millions of folks around the world.
Alas, I'm not one of them!**

It was just an ordinary trip from Los Angeles to Denver in the late 1980s. Unfortunately, I missed my flight and had to hang out at the airport until the next flight, which was three hours later. With so much time to kill, I bought a mindless paperback at a kiosk, plunked myself down at a café, ordered a coffee, and began to read.

Time passed. People came and went. About an hour into my wait, I happened to notice several handsome young men gathered a few tables away. Not only were they well-dressed in khaki pants and dark blue blazers, they were also extremely well-behaved. Before long, I caught several of them looking back at me, but didn't give it much thought. After all, I looked a tad off-center in western attire complete with cowboy boots and a Stetson hat. I had dressed that way in anticipation of doing some horseback riding in Denver.

More time passed, and I continued reading my book, so I barely noticed when one of those good-looking guys walked over and took a seat at my table. Neither one of us said a word for a moment. Finally, he spoke up. "Hi. How's your day going?"

"Fine. How's yours going?" I answered, glancing up, thinking that he was a bit young to be flirting with me.

"It's fine. Oh, I'm James, part of the group over there," he said, proudly indicating the men behind him. "By the way, do you know that you're sitting at our lucky table?"

"*Your* lucky table?" I responded, bewildered.

"Yeah. You see, we all sit around these four tables together before boarding our plane for a game. It's a tradition, sort of a lucky charm. But we can't right now because *you're* sitting here."

Completely confused now, and a bit annoyed, I asked, "Who is '*we*'?"

He looked at me in astonishment, then said with pride, "We're the Raiders!"

"Of what, the Lost Ark?" I answered sarcastically.

"The Los Angeles Raiders," he said, plainly stunned that I didn't know who the Raiders were.

Finally, it dawned on me. "The football team?"

"Yeah! That's us."

"And you want me to move to another table. Is that it?"

"It would mean a lot to us. We'll pay for your coffee, or even a dessert if you want one."

I threw back my head and let out a loud chuckle. "No problem."

He gave me a broad smile and turned to give his buddies a thumbs-up. Several Raiders immediately came to my table, grabbed my coffee and luggage, and carefully carried everything over to a nearby table, all the while thanking me as if I had just given them a million dollars.

I had just settled back into my book when one of their group, a slightly older but equally handsome guy, leaned on the chair next to me and asked, "May I join you?"

Thoroughly amused by all that had transpired, I replied, "Why not? Obviously, I need to learn a few things about football."

Sitting down, he introduced himself as one of the Raiders coaches, and informed me they were on their way to Houston to play a game. Genuinely, but with a touch of humor, he said, "My boys just got a good old-fashioned lesson in humility. It's probably the first time somebody didn't know who they were. Thank you."

"I don't know if that's a compliment or an insult, but I'll take it," I answered. "How did they choose who would tell me I was sitting at their lucky table?"

"Most of them volunteered, but I chose James. He's low-key and not aggressive."

"Good choice. He was very cute," I agreed.

"I won't tell him you said that. Raiders never want to be defined as cute. Now, tell me about you."

Thus began one of the most pleasant hours I've ever spent with a total stranger. It wasn't long before he invited me to come to Houston with the team. He would arrange for a room in Houston and a front-row seat at the game.

"Have you ever seen a football game?" he asked.

"No, never. Well, only on television with my father if I couldn't escape."

"Hey, why not give it a try? You'll love it. It's exciting. The guys would love it. You'd be their lucky charm. You're even dressed for Texas," he said, grabbing my Stetson hat from the table and plopping it on his head.

He was flirting, but so was I. What a temptation. But my Denver itinerary was in place, and I felt I couldn't just jump on a plane going in the opposite direction and abandon my hostess waiting there for me. It was such a tempting offer. And yes, in my senior moments I often regret that decision.

Fortuitously, for one and all—in numerous ways—the Raiders flight was announced. After one last plea from the coach to join them, off they all went.

The next day I read about the game in *The Denver Post*. The Raiders won. And all because I let them sit at their lucky table.

The Roman Drift

"It's not a small world. It's a closet, not even a walk-in one!"

In the mid-1970s I was romantically involved with William B. Murray, a talented writer and the love of my life. We met at the Melrose Theatre, where I was cast in a successful play he had written, *The Kitty Genovese Story*. We were soon, as the saying goes, "an item." Bill was quite versatile in that he wrote screenplays, books, plays, and fascinating articles for elite newspapers and magazines. He was half-Italian and half Irish, but definitely more the former in that he was fluent in Italian, adored Italy, and was an avid opera fan. He had even studied to be an opera singer in Italy during his younger years. He was the official translator for the Pirandello estate. It wasn't surprising when *Playboy* magazine offered him a one-year contract to be the American Editor of the Italian version of *Playboy*, to be published in Rome.

It was an exciting opportunity for both of us. Lawyers and agents met, and a contract was drawn up. All our living expenses in Rome were to be paid by *Playboy*, as well as all first-class travel expenses. The latter applied mainly to me, as Bill made it very clear that I was a working actress and had to go back and forth between Rome and Los Angeles in order to maintain an up-and-coming career.

Within weeks we jetted off to the Eternal City, where a small, charming apartment was waiting for us just off the famous Via Veneto, walking distance to the *Playboy* office. I immediately got an Italian agent and enrolled in a crash course in Italian. It was a six-week course, six hours a day, five days a week. Within a week, four of the eight students enrolled dropped out, leaving three bilingual students and me. Having no ear for languages, I was of course the dummy in the class, although somehow or other I got through it. Bill delighted in telling everyone that I had created a whole new language. After the course was finished, I was feeling a little homesick, and decided to briefly head back to Los Angeles to pursue one or two acting jobs before returning to Rome.

No sooner had I settled back into our Los Angeles bungalow when I received a call from the Melrose Theatre about doing another play there. The Melrose in the mid-1970s was an equity waiver theater, meaning it was limited to ninety-nine seats. It was considered one of the best small theatres in Los Angeles. Shows usually ran Thursdays through Sundays for several weekends. Membership was comprised of a great group of professional and wannabe actors all working together for the same goal: a successful Hollywood career.

The theater was going to showcase an evening of three generations of love, starting with *The Apple Tree*, the delightful Broadway musical that had opened in 1966 and which starred Barbara Harris, Alan Alda, and Larry Blyden. I was to appear in the first act, written by Mark Twain, in the pivotal role of Eve in the "The Diary of Adam and Eve," set in the Garden of Eden.

It was an abridged version, minus the original production's music and serpent.

The timing was perfect. The show was a trial run and scheduled to last for just two long weekends. Soon, I'd be back in Rome. Rehearsals were exhausting, not only because it was a two-person play, but because the director was one of my least-favorite persons and openly disliked the script. He kept saying, "It's fluff."

I'd counter, "It's written by Mark Twain and ran on Broadway."

Opening night validated my perspective. The performance was greeted with the sweet sound every actor craves: loud, sustained, rapturous applause. Being a trial run, newspaper reviewers had not been not invited, but word of mouth ensured that the theater was packed with happily entertained patrons at each performance.

I could have basked in those cheers for months, but before I could blink the run came to an end. After the wrap party, I went home, packed my bags, and made ready to jet to Rome the following day. While I would miss Los Angeles, my true love and my true home were now in the land of *la dolce vita*.

The flight to Rome was long and arduous, made more tiring because I'd had no time to rest after the show. Bill met me at the airport in Fiumicino, where we promptly staged a Technicolor-worthy romantic reunion that tested the limits of legality and public behavior, before speeding home to our private love nest. Sometime later, Bill told me about an important business dinner engagement we had to attend that evening. It was for a *Playboy* article on Italian movie stars, among them Franco Nero, renowned for his acting talent and machismo, and for being one of the world's hottest sex symbols. This was alright by me.

At eight o'clock we found ourselves at Nino's, an elegant restaurant near the Spanish Steps, with a small group of Italian show-biz folks, including Signore Nero. As we waited for our table, Bill introduced me around, and everyone graciously said, "*Buonasera. Benvenuti a Roma.*" After that, no one made any effort to communicate with me, in either English or Italian, although due to my travel fatigue, even my faulty Italian was not up to scratch. They all went on chatting in rapid Italian as though I was invisible. Bill was busy doing his journalistic thing, but would occasionally wink at me. I ordered a second and third glass of wine and began to take in the room.

I noticed two young American women seated by the window. (One can always spot Americans in Rome.) They seemed fascinated by our group, but kept pointing directly at me. They were, in fact, openly studying me. After a while, the wine kicked in, and I bravely walked over to their table. "You two seem to be staring at me. Is there something about me that's troubling you?"

The younger woman looked down for a moment, then said shyly, "Weren't you the star of *The Apple Tree* at the Melrose Theatre in Los Angeles last week?"

To say I was stunned would be an understatement. For a moment, I was as mute as the statue of the Virgin Mary standing atop the Column of the Immaculate Conception a short distance away. When I appeared in *The Apple Tree* I had shoulder-length dark hair and was dressed in a simple, form-fitted nude T-shirt with matching underwear and no shoes. Here in Rome, I still had the long dark hair, but was dressed in a stylish outfit and boots.

"Yes, yes, that was me," I stammered, having recovered my voice. Trying to be gracious, I said, "I hope you liked the show."

"We loved it. You were wonderful. You were the perfect Eve!" My newfound fans raved on and on about the show. Following mutual introductions, I thanked them for their kind comments and rejoined Bill's Italian group.

Judging from their expressions, it was obvious they had overheard part of the conversation. The ice had broken, the tide had turned, and the smart, sophisticated Romans looked at me with new interest. I was somebody, not just a Hollywood starlet, but a respected and well-known actress from Los Angeles. Suddenly, they were able to speak English, or at least broken English. Franco Nero, superstar of *Camelot* (1967), spaghetti westerns, eurocrime, and European art films, began to flirt with me in a most charming manner. One of the women kept telling me how *bella* I was. Another man asked if I had an acting agent in Rome. He subsequently arranged for a well-respected Italian agent to represent me in Italy.

Turns out Bill's attractive lady friend wasn't just another Hollywood starlet. She was somebody in her own right, a respected and well-known actress from Los Angeles. *Ciao, bella!*

BIOS

SANDRA de BRUIN

Sandra de Bruin has appeared in more than 100 television shows, including The F.B.I. *(1965–1974),* Ironside *(1967–1975),* Emergency *(1972–1979),* Cannon *(1971–1976),* The Carol Burnett Show *(1967–1978),* Law and Order *(1990–2010),* Three's Company *(1976–1984), six* Barnaby Jones *(1973–1980), five* The Rockford Files *(1974–1980),* Lou Grant *(1977–1982),* Quincy, M.E. *(1976–1983),* Knots Landing *(1979–1993),* ER *(1994–2009)—not to mention being a cast member of The Mighty Carson Art Players on* The Tonight Show Starring Johnny Carson *(1962–1992). Her credits also include several major films, more than a few Los Angeles stage productions, numerous commercials, work in voice-over and looping . . . and, yes, dancing in a production at the Los Angeles Music Center. These and many other show business adventures are included in this book.*

Sandra created the highly successful *Actor's Audition Log* as well as the *Performer's Workshop Log* to fulfill the organizational needs of her fellow performers. Her informative and witty articles have appeared in several magazines, and her scripts have been optioned, bought, sold—and dropped—by major studios and independent producers alike.

DEAN BRIERLY

Dean Brierly is a film historian and writer who has contributed to numerous print and online magazines, including *Cinema Retro, Filmfax, Outré, Sky*, and others. Among his many celebrity interviews are Gordon Parks, David Carradine, Michael Moriarty, Stella Stevens, Fred Williamson, and Joe Dante. He has contributed liner notes for Blu-ray and DVD releases, and publishes several film blogs, including Fifties Crime Films and Classic Hollywood Quotes. He is an exhibited photographer and is currently the Editor-in-Chief of *Black & White*, the fine art photography magazine. Dean has also worked in academic and corporate publishing environments.

INDEX

Made in United States
North Haven, CT
17 January 2023

31186009R00124